The

END

of the

WORLD

ACCORDING *to*

JESUS

of

NAZARETH

JEFF KINLEY

HARVEST PROPHECY
AN IMPRINT OF HARVEST HOUSE PUBLISHERS

Published in association with William K. Jensen Literary Agency, 119 Bampton Court, Eugene, Oregon 97404

Cover design by Bryce Williamson

Cover images © OMG Snap, Livinskiy / Adobe Stock; Roman Kulinskiy, Denis Torkhov, sergio34, John Theodor / Getty Images

Interior design by KUHN Design Group

For bulk, special sales, or ministry purchases, please call 1-800-547-8979.
Email: Customerservice@hhpbooks.com

This logo is a federally registered trademark of The Hawkins Children's LLC. Harvest House Publishers, Inc., is the exclusive licensee of this trademark.

The End of the World According to Jesus of Nazareth

Copyright © 2024 by Jeff Kinley
Published by Harvest House Publishers
Eugene, Oregon 97408
www.harvesthousepublishers.com

ISBN 978-0-7369-8868-1 (pbk)
ISBN 978-0-7369-8869-8 (eBook)

Library of Congress Control Number: 2023947079

Printed in the United States of America

24 25 26 27 28 29 30 31 32 / BP / 10 9 8 7 6 5 4 3 2 1

This book is dedicated to three dear friends,
mentors, and scholars—

Dr. Ed Hindson
Dr. Mark Hitchcock
Dr. Tommy Ice

—men whose enduring legacies in ministry and teaching
are a testament to their deep love for our Lord.

CONTENTS

WHAT'S SO IMPORTANT ABOUT JESUS' OLIVET DISCOURSE?

I t's the end of the world as we know it."

That's what a lot of people have been saying lately.

This concept is known by many names: the Apocalypse. Judgment Day. Armageddon. Doomsday. Cataclysmic Annihilation. The Extinction Event. *The End of the World.*

Different names. Same idea.

But more than a trendy catchphrase, the prospect of our world coming to an end is more like a foreboding spirit and is actually quite serious. It's like there's something in the air telling us we're getting precariously near closing time. It's the collective sense that humanity is racing toward the final hour. That it's Earth's "last call" before things shut down for good.

Apocalypse is in the air. Like the cartoon I recently saw depicting a long-haired and bearded man clothed in a prophet's garb, wearing a large sign that read, The End is *Near.* Following closely behind him was a similarly dressed man carrying his own sign that said, *I'm* the End.

All around us—from politicians to pundits to preachers—we're hearing the same refrain repeated: The human race and planet Earth are dancing dangerously close to some sort of cataclysmic precipice of destruction. In fact, even the most secular voices are now forecasting a bleak future, including those who release what is called Bulletin of the Atomic Scientists. Each year since the dropping of nuclear weapons during World War 2, these experts have gauged and evaluated just how close they believe humanity is to a global extinction event through what they call "The Doomsday Clock."

In January 2022, they posted this headline:

At Doom's Doorstep:
It is 100 Seconds to Midnight[1]

This headline marked the closest proximity to destruction they've ever set and is their most dramatic proclamation to date. In 2023, they moved the clock to 90 seconds to midnight. In 2024, they stated that it was still at 90 seconds. These bleak predictions underscore what they perceive as a potential series of existential threats to mankind that could result in a global catastrophic collapse and the end of civilization as we know it. They warn that unless we fundamentally alter our path, doomsday is inevitable and unavoidable. Among the threats they list are nuclear risks, bioweapons, famine, pandemics, and of course, climate change.

Almost everyone agrees that we are in an era of global crisis. Just consider where we are for a moment. We are living in an age saturated with wars, injustice, male governmental leaders identifying as women, human trafficking, out-of-control spending, irrecoverable debt, economic meltdowns, rampant immorality, the continual mass slaughter of innocent babies, and the death knell of reason and truth. It seems that we have grown accustomed to a global undercurrent of fear that lingers among us like a low-grade fever.

All this makes one wonder: Could humanity be a doomed race? Is this it? And if so, just how long will it be before this ship goes under for good? Though atheists and Bible-believers disagree as to the first cause of our origin, both argue that Earth and mankind did have a beginning. We just differ on how the beginning began and how the end will or could end.

How long before the bottom drops out and we plunge irreversibly into a bottomless pit of chaos and despair? Are we today literally seeing the "handwriting on the wall"? What will prove to be the tipping point—the final straw that breaks and sends us plummeting into the abyss? And most importantly, how are we to cope in the midst of this multifaceted pandora's box of threatening calamities?

Yes, Earth is a planet in peril, and we are walking on the textbook definition of thin ice.

But does any of this really matter to us? Does it really impact our daily lives and families? Should we care…*that much*? After all, why dwell on this subject? And why even talk about the end of the world— a morbid, dark, depressing, seemingly unnecessary, and mostly *irrelevant* prospect? Why write an entire book discussing such a distasteful and disturbing topic when we are already occupied with surviving perpetual pandemics, fearing wars, fighting inflation, and trying to forage for some personal meaning in the midst of an already-messed-up age? Why add to our anxiety by obsessing over future doomsday scenarios? Isn't that counterproductive?

The answer, of course, is yes.

However, at the same time, neither can any thinking person afford to simply dismiss or ignore the subject altogether, and here's a major reason why:

Jesus Christ spoke about the end times, and in great detail.

For that reason alone, we cannot merely pass off the "last days" as some faith-based fantasy or Christian conspiracy theory.

For those who claim Christ as Savior (and for everyone else as well), this is simply not an option. As we will see, the crises that currently seem oceans away in distance and time may reach our shores (and lives) much sooner than we anticipate. Rather than fading into our memory like last year's Super Bowl winner, the end times is a topic that, according to the Bible, simply isn't going away. On an almost daily basis, we are confronted by global developments in government, morality, religion, and geopolitics that constantly remind us we are well down the path to prophetic fulfillment as described in Scripture.

Everyone acknowledges that life here on earth will end at some point in the future. But according to Jesus of Nazareth, it won't be due to some rogue meteor, global warming, or an international thermonuclear meltdown. Just a few days prior to his crucifixion, Christ gathered with a small group of his disciples on the Mount of Olives just outside Jerusalem. There, he laid out God's prophetic plan for the end of days. And if he is right about earth's last days, wouldn't it be smart to know just *how* it will play out *before* it happens?

Fortunately, the rest of Scripture also harmonizes with Jesus' definitive narrative for the end of the world. In fact, it is repeatedly addressed, described, and prophesied in meticulous detail and in multiple places.

So to bring it a bit closer to home, wouldn't you like to know whether the apocalyptic events described in the Bible could occur in your lifetime? If the present global shifts and trajectory of current world events signify that we may be very near to the close of history as portrayed in the Bible, wouldn't you want to know? What if there was credible evidence to suggest that the beginning of the end was not centuries removed from us, but in reality, knocking at our front door?

Sounds a lot more relevant now, doesn't it?

However, instead of sensational speculation and wild, reckless predictions concerning future days of destruction, prudence dictates that we go straight to the source and see for ourselves. In this book, we will tackle the topic by considering the words of the One who claimed to be truth incarnate (John 14:6). We will consult him who alone prophesies history in advance.

In other words, we will let Christ himself tell us what's going to happen in his own unfiltered, unedited style.

Though this Jesus is not accessible by email, text, or Zoom call, he is nevertheless available, and he is able to speak directly to us through his written word, faithfully and accurately recorded in the Gospels. It is there on a hillside just outside Jerusalem where we are permitted to eavesdrop on a most interesting encounter between the Lord and his disciples. In a single sitting, the carpenter-rabbi-prophet reveals to them, and to us, the unparalleled prophetic narrative divinely destined to unfold in the last days. Apart from his gospel-saving message, it may prove to be the most valuable critical intel you've ever received. Compliments of Jesus of Nazareth.

Admittedly, a skeptical mind may object to the predictions of a first-century Jewish teacher. After all, just who is this Jesus of Nazareth that he should be qualified to speak on such topics, and do so some 2,000 years ago? Granted, he is universally seen as a good, kind, and loving man, but what valid reasons do we have to believe him regarding the future? Why trust *his* version of end-times events?

Fair enough.

With that in mind, before catapulting ourselves into Jesus' version of the last days, it makes sense to first examine the man himself. What kind of person was he? What does the evidence suggest concerning him? And why would we, or anyone, embrace his views, and stake our very lives on his prophecies concerning the future?

The answers to those questions are critical, for they will not only help shape our beliefs concerning the end times, but also decide our own destiny as well.

Jeff Kinley

PART I

WHO IS JESUS OF NAZARETH?

CHAPTER I

WHO IS JESUS OF NAZARETH?— HIS WORDS

One of the tragedies of the modern era is that we appear to have lost the art of critical thinking. With the explosion of information and knowledge available literally at our fingertips, we may nevertheless still be the least-informed generation in history. Students graduate high school, and even college, lacking the skills to read proficiently or to do basic math. Few today care to know or even understand history.[1] And it could be argued that critical thinking isn't the only skill we're losing. The basic ability to think and form rational thoughts is now at risk as well. Caught in a confusing haze somewhere between reality and online fantasy, I would argue that we're much better at *emoting* ("I feel like…") than we are at actual *thinking*. And many today who reject traditional values and ideas do so not because of factual data or rational reasons, but rather, because of how they *feel* about an issue or what the accepted mainstream narrative pressures them to believe or say.

Bottom line: We could use a lot more thinkers and true skeptics in our world. And that, curiously enough, brings us to Jesus and his prophecies concerning the end of days.

Admittedly, a skeptical mind might naturally object to the apocalyptic predictions of a first-century Jewish rabbi. Again, just who is this Jesus of Nazareth that he should be credibly qualified to speak on such topics, and for his words to still have relevance some 2,000 years later?

In this chapter and the next, we'll take an unfiltered look at this Jesus of Nazareth—his words, his works, and his person. From this we will address reasonable skepticism, answer important questions, understand more fully who he is, and learn why his prophecies concerning the end of the world can be trusted.

First, it must be acknowledged that no credible source today denies the historicity of Jesus Christ. Gone are the days when the "Jesus myth" could be argued. As early as AD 52, nonbiblical accounts were written attesting to the reality of Jesus' life and death.[2] Those sources include the pagan historian Thallus (AD 52), the Roman historian Tacitus (AD 56–120), a Syrian philosopher named Mara Bar-Serapion (AD 70), Pliny the Younger (AD 61–113), Suetonius (AD 69–140), and the famous Jewish historian Josephus (AD 37–101).

Though stopping short of subscribing themselves to Jesus' teaching, they all unanimously acknowledged his undeniable existence, documenting it for the ages.

WHAT HE SAID

As a teacher and communicator, Jesus Christ was unequaled. Though he never penned a manuscript, his teachings have inspired millions of books to be written. He was the master teacher, the quintessential communicator. But why? What made him so effective? How did he teach? And what was the impact of those teachings on his followers? Let's look then at ten ways Jesus' words and teaching were unique.

1. His Words Were Authoritative (Mark 1:22)

When Jesus taught, he did so with a sense of divine confidence. This was a stark contrast to the established religious leaders and influencers of his day. So fresh and rich were his words that multitudes were described as being "amazed at His teaching" (Matthew 7:28-29; Mark 1:22). The word "amazed" (Greek *ekplesso*) means "to strike a person out of his senses"—like being awestruck, shocked, or beside oneself. In short, Jesus brought the *wow factor* in his teaching, not because of some dramatic presentation method or due to his rugged handsome looks. On the contrary, Isaiah reminds us of how ordinary he looked, writing, "He has no stately form or majesty that we should look upon Him, nor appearance that we should be attracted to Him" (Isaiah 53:2).

Because of his authoritative speech, Jesus' audiences were left speechless; they were "hanging on to every word He said" (Luke 19:48).

2. His Words Were Challenging (Matthew 5-7; Luke 14:25-35; John 6:1-66)

Jesus' words and message confronted the status quo of his day. Concerning one's relationship with God, he challenged his listeners to rise above the accepted standards to achieve a new, deeper, more meaningful level of spirituality. The problem, he argued, was not primarily with one's external behavior, but rather, with the condition of the heart (Mark 7:18-23). By contrast, the religious leaders of his time measured a person's spiritual worth and merit based solely on external deeds committed or omitted. Jesus turned that idea inside out.

Jesus was never content to merely draw a big crowd (as some measure success in our day). Instead, he would often purposefully "weed out" those who were merely curious or casual in their commitment to him. And when he did so, he was met with opposition and mass withdrawal (John 6:66).

His words were challenging and demanding in that he asked his followers to be willing to love him above all other earthly relationships, even above the love of one's own life (Luke 14:26). This devotion he demanded even included a willingness to die for him (verse 27). In fact, he required his disciples to surrender their concept of life itself to him and to submit their wills to his. Essentially, Christ challenged them to sign over the title deed of their souls to him and him alone (Matthew 10:38-39). Unless they did these things, Jesus boldly asserted, they simply could not be his disciples (Luke 14:26-27, 33-34). We can understand why he cautioned the crowds to count the cost before deciding to follow him (verses 28-32).

As the self-proclaimed Son of God, Jesus was willing to lay it all on the line for his Father, and he expected the same sacrifice from those who claimed him as their Lord (Matthew 10:24; John 15:18-25; 17:14, 18). If these same challenging words of Christ were proclaimed and preached more in churches today, would they empty them, or would a new breed of bold and courageous disciples be unleashed upon the world? And how much different would our culture be?

3. His Words Were Life-Changing (John 6:68)

Jesus' teaching did far more than just fill people's heads with knowledge. Instead, they imparted life itself. As Simon Peter confessed, "You have words of eternal life" (John 6:68). Due in part to his teaching, Christ's followers came to believe and know that he was "the Holy One of God" (verse 69). Among some of his life-altering words were these:

> Ask, and it will be given to you; seek, and you will find; knock, and it will be opened to you (Matthew 7:7).

> Truly, truly, I say to you, unless one is born again he cannot see the kingdom of God (John 3:3).

> Do not worry then, saying, "What will we eat?" Or "What will we drink?" Or "What will we wear for clothing?" For

the Gentiles eagerly seek all these things; for your heavenly Father knows that you need all these things. But seek first His kingdom and His righteousness, and all these things will be added to you. So do not worry about tomorrow; for tomorrow will care for itself. Each day has enough trouble of its own (Matthew 6:31-34).

What does it profit a man to gain the whole world, and forfeit his soul? For what will a man give in exchange for his soul? (Mark 8:36-37).

You have heard that it was said, "You shall love your neighbor and hate your enemy." But I say to you, love your enemies and pray for those who persecute you (Matthew 5:43-44).

Words of eternal life.

4. His Words Gave Hope (Matthew 11:28-30)

Christ appeared at a time when the Jewish people were not only under subjugation to a pagan Roman government, but also were weighed down by the extrabiblical religious laws created by the ruling religious leaders—the Pharisees and Sadducees. Because of this, his message included words that imparted much-needed hope to those who heard him. In that context, consider the following hope-infused offerings he gave to his people:

Come to Me, all who are weary and heavy-laden, and I will give you rest. Take My yoke upon you and learn from Me, for I am gentle and humble in heart, and you will find rest for your souls. For My yoke is easy and My burden is light (Matthew 11:28-30).

All authority has been given to Me in heaven and on earth. Go therefore and make disciples of all the nations, baptizing them in the name of the Father and the Son and the Holy Spirit, teaching them to observe all that I commanded you; and lo, I am with you always, even to the end of the age (Matthew 28:18-20).

I am the bread of life; he who comes to Me will not hunger, and he who believes in Me will never thirst (John 6:35).

The thief comes only to steal, and kill, and destroy; I came that they might have life, and have it abundantly. I am the good shepherd; the good shepherd lays down his life for the sheep (John 10:10).

My sheep hear My voice, and I know them, and they follow Me; and I give eternal life to them, and they will never perish; and no one will snatch them out of My hand. My Father, who has given them to Me, is greater than all; and no one is able to snatch them out of the Father's hand. I and the Father are one (John 10:27-30).

I am the resurrection and the life; he who believes in Me will live even if he dies (John 11:25).

Let not your heart be troubled; believe in God, believe also in Me. In My Father's house are many dwelling places; if it were not so, I would have told you; for I go to prepare a place for you. If I go to prepare a place for you, I will come again and receive you to Myself, that where I am, there you may be also (John 14:1-3).

These things I have spoken to you, so that in Me you may have peace. In the world you have tribulation, but take courage; I have overcome the world (John 16:33).

Words of hope that are still true for you today.

5. His Words Were Powerful (Mark 4:35-41)

Obviously, anyone can speak in grandiose, braggadocios language. But not everyone utters speech that actually suspends the laws of nature and the universe, altering both physical and chemical realities. Consider that, with a word, Jesus...

- transformed water into fermented wine (John 2:1-11)

- calmed a violent storm (Mark 4:35-41)

- healed the lame and those with leprosy (John 5:1-9; Mark 1:40-45)

- commanded supernaturally endowed demons to flee (Mark 1:21-28)

- cursed a fig tree (Matthew 21:18-19; Mark 11:12-14)

- raised the dead (Luke 7:11-17; John 11:1-44)

Keep in mind that the circumstances surrounding these occurrences and the environments in which they took place prevent them from being explained away as mere mind tricks, sleight of hand, misdirection, or illusionary magic. No, the aforementioned miracles Jesus performed (all originating solely from the words out of his mouth) were corroborated and verified by multiple eyewitness accounts. And as his own disciples noted, "Who then is this, that even the wind and the sea obey him?" (Mark 4:41). Who indeed? What kind of person can alter chemical compositions, control the climate and physical environments, cure organic diseases, reverse the effects of muscular atrophy, create from nothing perfectly cooked food, shut down the forces of nature, and bring back to life a person who is confirmed to be dead? The answer to these questions brings us closer to the true identity of this carpenter from Nazareth.

6. His Words Were Prophetic (Matthew 26:2)

Those today who claim to be able to predict the future are a dime a dozen. Throughout history, there has been no shortage of self-proclaimed prophets and wannabe prognosticators. So, what makes Jesus' predictions different? What sets his prophetic words apart from all the rest? And what distinguishes him from a palm reader, an astrological horoscope, or a random fortune cookie? Two undeniable facts: (1) His prophecies were specific, and (2) They all came true, literally and exactly as he predicted.

Jesus, during his earthly ministry, accurately prophesied all the following:

- that one of his disciples would betray him (Matthew 26:21-22; Luke 22:47-48)

- that all his disciples would forsake him (Matthew 26:31-32, 56)

- that Peter would deny him three times (Matthew 26:33-34, 74-75)

- that he would suffer at the hands of the religious rulers (Matthew 16:21; Luke 22:63-65)

- the place of his death (Matthew 16:21; Mark 15:40-41)

- the manner of his death (Matthew 26:2; Mark 15:26-27)

- the time of his death (Matthew 26:2; John 19:14-16)

- his resurrection from the dead on the third day (John 2:18-22; Matthew 16:21; 27:62-63; 28:6)

- that Mary of Bethany would be immortalized (Matthew 26:11-13)

- the coming of the Holy Spirit (John 14:26; Acts 2:1-4)

- the destruction of Jerusalem (Luke 19:43-44; 21:20)

- the destruction of the Jewish temple (Matthew 24:1-2)

- the scattering of the Jewish people to all the nations (Luke 21:24)

- the future, ongoing domination of Jerusalem by the Gentiles until the last days (Luke 21:24)

- the persecution of the Jewish people (Luke 23:28-30)

- the preservation of the Jewish people (Luke 21:24)

Without question, every one of those prophecies came to pass just as Jesus predicted. With this stellar track record of success in mind, are there any other prophecies Jesus made that have yet to be fulfilled? Yes.

- He prophesied concerning both specific and major catastrophic global events and occurrences that will materialize during the last days (Matthew 24:1-41; Mark 13:1-37; Luke 21:5-19, 25-38)

- He prophesied he would one day return for his disciples (John 14:1-3)

- He prophesied his visible return to planet Earth to judge the nations and to redeem national Israel (Matthew 24:29-31; 25:31-46)

And as we will see in the coming chapters, Jesus made scores of other predictions that describe what will happen during Earth's final days.

All this concrete evidence proves that Jesus was way more than some sort of "Nazarene Nostradamus." Far from it, for not a single prophetic word spoken by him has failed to come true so far. Because of this, we have every reason to confidently believe that every yet-to-be-fulfilled prophecy will also come to pass. Therefore, this begs the question: What kind of man can do such a thing? And with such pinpoint accuracy? Who could really know the future so perfectly except the one who orchestrates it?

7. *His Words Were Controversial/Offensive (Matthew 23:1-36)*

Like no one before him, Jesus of Nazareth never backed down from declaring the truth. Specifically, he confronted the spiritual state of Israel, most notably through his scalding rebuke of the Jewish religious leaders. In Matthew 23, his words condemning both their leadership and their character are well documented.

In that sermon, he boldly declared them to be

- self-righteous (verses 1-5)
- self-promoting (verses 6-7)
- roadblocks keeping others from entering heaven (verse 13)
- hell-bound (verses 13, 33)
- legalists, false leaders (verse 15)
- blind guides (verses 16, 17, 18, 24)
- fools (verse 17)
- hypocrites (verses 23, 25, 27, 29)
- murderers (verses 31-32, 34-35)
- serpents, vipers (verse 33)
- hinderers of the truth (Luke 11:52)

Clearly, Jesus wasn't intent on winning a popularity contest or garnering favor with the powerful elite.

Can you imagine someone publicly confronting respected religious or political figures like this today? And on their own turf? It's no wonder that, when the Jewish religious leaders heard his words, they were deeply offended and insulted (Luke 11:45). And so much so that they became hostile toward him, plotting against him (Luke 11:53-54), eventually devising a plan to kill him (Matthew 12:14; John 11:45-53). And yet this, too, Jesus prophesied would happen (Mark 10:33-34).

Christ was not afraid to stir up controversy through speaking the truth. And he was not intimidated by those in power.

8. *His Words Were Eternal (Matthew 24:35)*

This falls under the category of "things Christ claimed." And yet, given the evidence we already have concerning the divine nature of his words, it seems reasonable. Jesus claimed his words would outlast the existing heaven and earth (Matthew 24:35). Long after this present world has been destroyed and incinerated with intense heat (2 Peter 3:10), Jesus' words will still be around. Put another way, even the universe is temporary, but Christ's words will live forever (Matthew 5:18; Mark 13:31; Luke 21:33).

9. *His Words Were True (John 18:37)*

Jesus unapologetically claimed to be the embodiment of truth itself (John 14:6). If this assertion is valid, it follows that all his words would be true as well. At the end of his earthly life, he confidently stated to his Father that he had given his disciples only the truth, which was the Word of God (John 17:14, 17). He further declared that his words had made them spiritually "clean" (John 15:3; 13:10; cf. Ephesians 5:26). One of his closest followers, and perhaps the one who knew him best, later wrote that Jesus was "full of grace and *truth*" (John 1:14).

10. *His Words Declared Himself to Be God (John 8:58)*

This is the most direct and divine of all Jesus' professions concerning himself. And he made similar statements on other occasions. Though some will assert that Jesus never specifically claimed to be God, the Gospel writers tell a different story.

In John 8:56-58, Jesus claimed to predate Abraham (2000 BC), identifying himself as the great "I AM" (Yahweh) of Exodus 3:14. And how do we know this is what he meant? Because the Jews immediately "picked up stones to throw at Him" (John 8:59). This was in accordance with the command to stone someone to death for the sin of blasphemy (Leviticus 24:16). In John 5:17-18, Jesus specifically makes himself to be "equal with God" (see also Revelation 1:8).

On another occasion, during winter and the festival of Hannukah, the people surrounded Jesus, asking him to plainly tell them whether he was the promised Messiah. He replied:

> *I told you, and you do not believe*; the works that I do in My Father's name, these testify of Me. But you do not believe because you are not of My sheep. My sheep hear My voice, and I know them, and they follow Me; and *I give eternal life to them*, and they will never perish; and no one will snatch them out of My hand (John 10:25-28).

Obviously, imparting eternal life to someone is a prerogative belonging to God alone. And he follows up this claim with these words: "I and the Father are one" (verse 30). This undoubtedly qualifies as a self-declaration of deity. Christ claimed to be God incarnate and co-equal with the Father. He also affirmed the Christian doctrine of the Trinity, or the truth that God exists in three persons, yet one essence.

And how did Jesus' Jewish hearers understand these claims? What was their response to these deity-laced words? As previously noted, they "took up stones again to stone Him" (John 10:31), stating, "For a good work we do not stone You, but for blasphemy; and because You, being a man, *make Yourself out to be God"* (verse 33).

Notice Jesus' reply to this was not to backpedal or to declare, "No, no. That's not what I meant at all. You totally misunderstood me." Instead, he doubled down on his claim, declaring that he was indeed the "Son of God" (verse 36) and that "the Father is in Me, and I in the Father" (verse 38). This assertion of unique oneness with God was never made by any other prophet in Scripture. And for good reason.

Jesus would later state in John 14:9 that "he who has seen Me has seen the Father," a direct claim that he was God incarnate.

In Matthew 11:27, Christ claimed to have exclusive and complete knowledge of the Father, something obviously only God himself would possess (see also John 8:19).

In Matthew 9:5-7, Jesus forgave sins that were committed against God, then authenticated his words by supernaturally healing the paralyzed man whose sins he had forgiven.

Without a doubt, Christ chose his words carefully, and was highly intentional about openly defining his relationship with the Father, distinguishing it from anyone else's.

These are some of Jesus' direct, overt verbal claims about himself. Let's look now at some additional concrete and undeniable ways he showed himself to be God.

CHAPTER 2

WHO IS JESUS OF NAZARETH?—HIS WORKS AND WITNESS

T oday, we find ourselves in a strange moment, living in a chaotic culture of confusion. The number of people choosing to personally "identify" as something other than what they actually are is growing exponentially. Men who think they're women. Boys who believe they are really girls who are trapped inside a male body, and vice versa. In the psychological phenomenon known as "furries," some are now identifying as cats, dogs, and even horses. And what's even more alarming than this mental illness is the fact that the culture, the government, hospitals, and universities are playing along with the delusion. It almost makes you long for the days when people would merely claim to be Napoleon or some other legendary figure from history. Occasionally, some people even claim to be Jesus. However, none of them ever live up to their hype.

Obviously, anyone can make ridiculous or grandiose claims concerning their identity. Proving those claims, however, is a different story. We've already seen how the real Jesus boldly asserted he was God Almighty. But how did he back up his declarations of deity?

We have documented a few of the miracles Jesus performed through his spoken word. But what are some other supernatural signs and wonders he openly performed? As it turns out, there are many, including these:

- He instantly produced food for up to 20,000 people at once (Matthew 14:14-21; John 6:5-13)

- He walked on water (Matthew 14:22-36; Mark 6:45-56)

- He cast out demons (Matthew 8:28-34)

- He healed incurable, internal diseases (Luke 8:43-48)

- He enabled the blind to see (Matthew 9:27-31; John 9:1-38)

- He enabled the mute to speak (Matthew 9:32-33)

- He recreated a withered hand, restoring it to full form and function (Matthew 12:10-13)

- He straightened a crooked body (Luke 13:10-17)

- He cured and cleansed ten lepers at once (Luke 17:11-19)

- He reattached and healed the cut-off ear of the high priest's servant (Luke 22:50-51)

All of Jesus' miraculous works not only had a practical benefit to individuals, but also served as credible, publicly verifiable evidence concerning who he claimed to be. His miracles backed up his words, serving as stand-alone testimony to the claim that he was indeed God in human flesh.

Of course, Jesus' capstone miracle was rising from the dead, just as he had earlier prophesied (Matthew 16:21; 17:22-23). And in doing so, he defeated humanity's greatest enemy, proving beyond any reasonable doubt he was exactly who he claimed to be (John 20:1-28).

Consider this: Any gifted speaker or charismatic persona can sway a crowd or persuade individuals concerning a proposed narrative. Trained, skilled presenters can master the art of communication, perform psychological mind tricks, and manipulate audiences toward specific beliefs or desired responses. Any good illusionist can fool a crowd. In fact, those well-versed in the power of suggestive speech or positive thinking can "cure" individuals of psychosomatic illnesses or temporarily mask the symptoms of a deeper physical or emotional problem. However, only a divine being can make withered, atrophied muscles disappear and, in their place, produce perfectly healthy tissue.

Only God can do that.

Only God can, in an instant, eradicate long-term disease.

Only God can suspend and replace the laws of physics.

Only God can truly resurrect the dead back to life.

Only God can predict the future with undeniable precision.

Only God has charge over nature, disease, demons, and death.

Guess what? Jesus of Nazareth did *all* those things.

THE WORDS AND WORKS OF JESUS

As we survey the words and works of Christ, it becomes clear that they collectively point to the same conclusion. This Nazarene was more than a carpenter. Indeed, he was more than a man, or even a prophet. Now let's look at what we can learn about his very nature.

The character of Jesus Christ, as evidenced by the preponderance of literary and historical evidence, is unparalleled in the annals of time. As we now examine who he was, the pieces of the puzzle come together to form a complete picture. Like a pixelated image coming into crystal-clear focus, the portrait that emerges is of one unlike any other—fully God and fully man. The God-man. In short, the person and character of Jesus Christ testify to him being God. The following are but a few of his multifaceted, extraordinary attributes.

1. Jesus was prophesied—his birth, including how and where he would be born, was divinely predicted 700 years prior to his incarnation (Isaiah 7:14; Micah 5:2).

2. His childhood was unique—as a young boy, Jesus grew in wisdom, strength, stature, and favor with God and man (Luke 2:40, 52). He was humble and inquisitive concerning the things of God (Luke 2:46). And yet, even at the young age of 12, he possessed a strong sense of his divine mission—so much so that his understanding and grasp of Scripture amazed even the aged, learned men of his day (Luke 2:47-50).

3. He was zealous for God's truth, all the way up to and throughout his arrest, trials, and execution (Psalm 69:9; Matthew 27:11; Mark 14:48-49, 62; Luke 22:67-70; John 2:12-25; 19:11).

4. He lived life as a humble servant to humanity, never wavering from his mission (Matthew 20:28; Mark 10:45; Philippians 2:5-11).

5. He consistently exhibited compassion and forgiveness to those whom his culture considered insignificant (Mark 1:40-42). He even extended forgiveness to his enemies and to those who murdered him (Luke 23:34).

6. He was without sin. Even the ones who hated him could find no legitimate fault in him (Luke 4:1-13; Hebrews 4:15; 1 Peter 2:22; 1 John 3:5).

7. He possessed the ability to relate to every person. Like all men, he was born of a woman (Galatians 4:4) and lived like we do, in human flesh (1 John 1:1; Romans 8:3). Similarly, he died as men do (Hebrews 2:9). But because he rose

from the dead, all those who place faith in him will also overcome death (John 11:25; Romans 6:4-5).

Due to the panorama of Jesus' earthly experience, there is no category of human experience with which he cannot identify, including

- hunger (Matthew 4:2)
- thirst (John 4:7; 19:28)
- fatigue (John 4:5-6)
- grief (Isaiah 53:3; Luke 19:41; John 11:35)
- temptation (Luke 4:1-13; Hebrews 4:15)
- development and growth (physical, emotional, social, spiritual—Luke 2:52; Jesus was at one time a toddler, preteen, and teenager)
- disappointment and desertion by friends (Matthew 26:36-50)
- despair (Matthew 26:38-39)
- extreme stress (Luke 22:41-44)
- anguish (Hebrews 5:7)
- dread (Matthew 20:22; Luke 22:42)
- physical abuse and torture (Matthew 27:29-30; John 19:1-3)
- abandonment (Matthew 27:46)
- denial (Matthew 26:36, 69-75)
- joy (Luke 10:21; Hebrews 1:8-9; 12:2)
- accomplishment (John 17:4; 19:30)

Because of these experiences, Jesus can identify with what you go through in your own life. He can say, "I know how you feel."

8. He was resolute and laser-focused in his mission of bringing salvation to mankind (Matthew 16:21; Luke 9:51). Jesus was intent on fulfilling his purpose in life. But he was much more than being merely "purpose driven." He was *divinely* driven to complete the work the Father had given him to accomplish (John 17:4).

9. He was fully dependent on the Father (John 4:34; 5:30; 6:38; 8:29). Nothing motivated Christ more than to align himself with the Father's will and to rest in his guidance, provision, and strength. As the God-man, he voluntarily subjected himself to the Father's will. For Jesus, this was an even higher priority than eating (John 4:34).

10. He was determined to persevere (Hebrews 12:1-4). Jesus never gave up. Motivated by the Father's plan and what awaited him beyond death (joy and his place at the Father's right hand), he "endured the cross, despising the shame" (and the pain). Nothing would deter Jesus from accomplishing salvation for those who would believe. Fatigue. Rejection. Disappointment. Dread. Beatings. And even the experience of the cross itself—undergoing excruciating pain and an eternity's worth of divine wrath and hell compacted into a six-hour period of time—even *this* did not deter him from finishing the work he was sent to do. Though he could have summoned 10,000 angels to rescue him from that torturous death, he allowed himself to be arrested, abused, and crucified (Matthew 26:53). And he did all that for *you*.

So, what can we deduce from all this? What conclusions might a thinking, reasonable person reach concerning Jesus? What was the conclusion of those to whom he ministered? Even better, what did the ones who lived and travelled with him say? Those companions who knew him best? The ones who saw more than the public Jesus, but walked and worked with him "backstage"? After all was said and done and the crowds had dispersed, what was their final evaluation? And what did those who anticipated his arrival prophesy concerning him? Consider the following testimonials:

- John—Jesus is the preexistent one, God (John 1:1-3; 1 John 3:16; 5:20)

- Thomas—Jesus is "My Lord and my God!" (John 20:28)

- The blind man—Jesus is Lord and worthy of worship (John 9:35-38)

- Peter—Jesus is both Lord and Christ (Acts 2:36)

- Paul—Jesus is the sovereign creator and sustainer of the universe, the Savior, Lord, and preeminent one, the one mediator between God and man (Acts 20:28; Philippians 2:5-6; Colossians 1:16-17; 1 Timothy 3:16; Titus 2:13)

- Author of Hebrews—Jesus is the exact representation of God (Hebrews 1:1-3)

Others who claim Jesus is God include:

- David—Matthew 22:43-45

- Isaiah—Isaiah 7:14; 9:6

- Jeremiah—Jeremiah 23:5-6

- Matthew—Matthew 1:23

- angels—Luke 2:11

- God the Father—Hebrews 1:8-10

Clearly, there has never been anyone in history like Jesus of Nazareth. He stands alone. Unmatched. Unrivalled. Unequalled. In fact, no historical or religious figure, king, military leader, or priest remotely comes close to him in conversation, conduct, or character. No one has ever been who Jesus Christ was and is.

No priest so holy.

No prophet so bold.

No king so humble.

No rabbi so wise.

No counselor so understanding.

No teacher so profound.

No friend so loyal.

No shepherd so protective.

No man so noble.

No son so obedient.

No example so worthy of following.

No God so near.

Because of this, every person who encounters the truth about this Jesus, as you have in these pages, must respond to the evidence presented. Each of us must decide how we will view him, what we believe about him, and how we will treat him in our minds and hearts.

Was Jesus merely a good man and nothing else? Ask yourself: Would a good man tell others he was God and that they should trust in him alone for their eternal destiny and salvation from hell? Would a good man do that? No. A deranged man? Perhaps. An evil, deceptive man? Likely. But contemplate how a deranged or devilish individual could possibly do what Jesus did. No mentally unstable person could consistently portray such perfect, Godlike character. And no deceiver or imposter would or could die for the sins of others, then miraculously rise from the dead within a few short days.

Assuredly, the resurrection of Jesus Christ is the final validation concerning his identity. For who can definitively and permanently conquer death but God alone?

BUCKLE UP

With such overwhelming evidence pointing to Christ being God, his prophetic and apocalyptic sermon in Matthew 24–25 now takes on a whole new level of meaning and significance for us. Rather than merely being the poetic ramblings of a first-century martyr on his way to arrest and execution, the Olivet Discourse now becomes a Rosetta Stone deciphering the last days for us.

In short, Jesus of Nazareth, the Son of God, is about to tell us exactly what is going to happen in the future.

And how the world will end.

PART 2

WHAT DID JESUS PROPHESY?

CHAPTER 3

JERUSALEM WILL BE DESTROYED

Matthew 24:1-2

It's a Wednesday in April in AD 33. Jesus Christ is in the last week of his earthly life and ministry. Just two days earlier, he had humbly but triumphantly ridden on a donkey into Jerusalem amid cheers of "Hosanna to the Son of David! Blessed is He who comes in the name of the LORD! Hosanna in the highest!" (Matthew 21:9; see also Mark 11:8-11; Luke 19:35-38). Because it was Passover week, thousands of Jewish pilgrims from around the known world had descended upon the holy city. But though multitudes cried out this messianic greeting, the Jewish leadership were becoming increasingly skeptical, unbelieving, and hostile toward the self-proclaimed Messiah.

The previous day, Jesus had entered the temple in the late afternoon, and after looking around, left with the Twelve for Bethany, a town about two-and-a-half miles east of Jerusalem (Mark 11:11; Luke 21:37).

On Tuesday, Jesus returns to Jerusalem, coming down from Bethany via the Mount of Olives. On his way, he becomes hungry and spots a fig tree in the distance. But when he arrives, he sees that while the fig tree has leaves, it has not yielded any fruit. He proceeds to curse the tree, condemning it to a lifetime of fruitlessness (Matthew 21:18-19; Mark 11:13-14). As the disciples would see, Israel herself also had plenty of "leaves" (promise, religious activity, busyness), but no "fruit" (spiritual life).

Once again ascending to the temple area, Jesus begins driving out those who were buying and selling, turning over the tables of the money changers (Matthew 21:12-13). Both of these groups were gouging the public, charging excessive fees. This is why Jesus called them "robbers" (verse 13). As a result, the chief priests and scribes began plotting how they might kill him (Mark 11:18; Luke 19:47).

Following this, Jesus heals the blind and the lame who had somehow made their way to the temple, most likely seeking a compassionate helping hand (Matthew 21:14; cf. Acts 3:2). Children run after him, hailing him as the Messiah (verses 15-16). He then returns to Bethany for the night (verse 17; Luke 21:37-38).

On Wednesday, Jesus returns to Jerusalem with the disciples, who see that the cursed fig tree has completely withered (verses 20-21). He enters the temple area and begins teaching. Confronted by the chief priests, the elders, the Pharisees, and the Sadducees, he responds to their questions, often with parables. He then delivers his most scathing rebuke of the Pharisees (Matthew 23:1-36; Mark 12:38-40; Luke 20:45-47). This was the last straw for them. Following this, he observes a widow placing her coins into the temple treasury (Mark 12:41-44; Luke 21:1-4).

IT'S ALL GONNA BURN

It is at this point, as he was leaving the temple, that Jesus' disciples marvel at the beauty of the temple and surrounding structures, remarking, "Teacher, behold what wonderful stones and what wonderful buildings!" (Mark 13:1). Luke adds that they were particularly enamored with how the temple was "adorned with beautiful stones and votive gifts" (Luke 21:5).

The structure they are referring to is commonly called Herod's temple because it was Herod I, the governor of Galilee, who had made the refurbishing and expansion of the temple buildings possible. A ruler of the Hasmonaean dynasty, King Herod (also called "king of the Jews") was a ruthless, unmerciful, and immoral man. In spite of this, he had aided the Jews by significantly adding to the size and grandeur of the second temple (Solomon's temple being the first, 950–586 BC). Herod began his construction projects on the temple and its accompanying structures in 20 BC, and the work wasn't finished until AD 64.

Dr. Randall Price provides helpful insight here:

> Herod secured his position as the proxy Jewish ruler under Roman occupation, dubbing himself "King Herod." Herod knew that in order to rule the Jewish people he would have to conform to traditional Jewish practices, so he converted to Judaism to appease the priests, and in 20 BC he proposed a renovation of the existing temple of Zerubbabel on a more magnificent scale.

> By the time of Herod, the second temple had suffered centuries of assault, repairs, and the general ravages of time. In making plans to reconstruct the temple, Herod had to follow the biblical design and legal requirements that govern the size of the building he could construct. However, Herod had other parties to please, and most important of these were the Roman authorities upon whom his right to rule depended. If his architectural projects could make Jerusalem a modern metropolis rivaling other Roman cities with a magnificent building that highlighted the classical tastes of the West, he could hope to retain Roman favor.[1]

Essentially, Herod sought to impress Rome while simultaneously appeasing the Jews.

For the Jews, the temple housed the presence of God in the Holy of Holies. The magnificent structure and surrounding buildings were a testament to the grandeur and glory of their God.

The votive gifts mentioned in Luke's account were donations that wealthy individuals gave to the temple. John MacArthur explains,

> Wealthy people gave gifts of gold sculpture, golden plaques, and other treasures to the temple. Herod had donated a golden vine with clusters of golden grapes nearly six feet tall. The gifts were displayed on the walls and suspended in the portico. They constituted an unimaginable collection of wealth. All of these riches were looted by the Romans when the temple was destroyed.[2]

Even today, some well-meaning churchgoers will make comments about the massive structures of churches, citing the millions of dollars in constructions costs, ornamental fixtures, gold-colored lamps, colossal columns, wings, outbuildings, athletic amenities, special chairs, and chandeliers—with many such features made possible by wealthy church members whose names are immortalized on plaques and nameplates. Some pastors and congregations even refer to their buildings as the "House of the Lord" or the "Lord's House," as if, like the Jewish temple, God's presence and glory resided there in some inner sanctum.

But we must remind ourselves that a church's "sanctuary" is simply a building where the actual church gathers each week. It's brick and mortar, sheet rock, wires, carpet, and wood. Further, no New Testament verse elevates such buildings to any special stature. Keep in mind that the early church met in homes (Acts 2:46; 12:12; 16:40; Romans 16:3, 5; Colossians 4:15; Philemon 1-2). Biblically, the church is *people*—you and me, and anyone who is indwelt by the Holy Spirit in this age. To combat and correct the aforementioned perpetuated misunderstanding, perhaps instead of saying, "See you at church on Sunday," we should say, "I will see you when the church gathers this Sunday."

However, to clarify, what Jesus says next to his disciples has less to do with material priorities and more with a specific prophecy concerning that beautiful temple and the Jewish people who worshipped there. Remember that just two days earlier, Christ had been hailed as the blessed Messiah, much to the disapproval of the Pharisees (Matthew 21:6-11; Mark 11:8-11; Luke 19:35-40). But as it turned out, the fickle crowds had exhibited only a thin veneer of worship and acceptance. Two days later, these worshippers were nowhere to be found. But this wasn't the first time that multitudes had deserted him, as Jesus had witnessed this kind of shallow faith before (John 6:1-66). By this point in Christ's ministry, the Jewish leaders had already officially rejected him as their prophesied Messiah and king. This is why, as Jesus approached the city that Monday afternoon, he wept over it, lamenting,

> If you had known in *this day*, even you, the things which make for peace! But now they have been hidden from your eyes. For the days will come upon you when your enemies will throw up a barricade against you, and surround you and hem you in on every side, and they will level you to the ground and your children within you, and they will not leave in you one stone upon another, because you did not recognize the *time of your visitation* (Luke 19:42-44).

In what is assuredly one of the saddest passages in all of Scripture, John succinctly wrote, "He was in the world, and the world was made through Him, and the world did not know Him. He came to His own, and those who were His own did not receive Him" (John 1:10-11).

The creation didn't recognize their own creator.

And the Jews didn't receive their own Messiah.

The next day, Tuesday, Jesus returns to the temple area and addresses the chief priests' and elders' questions, speaking in parables that signify their rejection of the kingdom of God. And that's when he delivers his most stinging rebuke and condemnation of the religious elite (Matthew 21:23–23:39). And yet, even in his condemnation of them, his heart was broken over their unwillingness to accept God's plan—and God's man—for them. It is at this time that Christ repeats a mournful prophecy he had given at an earlier point in his ministry:

> Jerusalem, Jerusalem, who kills the prophets and stones those who are sent to her! How often I wanted to gather your children together, the way a hen gathers her chicks under her wings, and you were unwilling. Behold, your house is being left to you desolate! For I say to you, from now on you will not see Me until you say, "Blessed is He who comes in the name of the Lord!" (Matthew 23:37-39; cf. Luke 13:34-35).[3]

This prophecy is significant, for at least three reasons:

1. It foreshadows the destruction of the Jewish temple, which occurred in AD 70 ("your house is being left to you desolate").

2. It prophesies the further extension of the period known as the "times of the Gentiles," which began in 586 BC with the destruction of Jerusalem and the temple by the Babylonian ruler Nebuchadnezzar (2 Kings 25:1-10; Jeremiah 39:1-10) and continues until the end of Antichrist's reign (Luke 21:24; Romans 11:25-26).

3. It forecasts the absence of Messiah in the life of Israel until they call upon him at the end of the age (Zechariah 12:10; Matthew 23:39; Romans 11:26).

Jesus was officially saying to the collective nation of Israel "Goodbye for now."

Of course, all of this was far removed from the disciples' minds that Wednesday afternoon as they pointed out the beauty and impressive structures of the temple.

A brief time gap occurs between Matthew 24:1 and verse 3. In verse 1, Jesus and the disciples are just leaving the temple area. But by the time we get to verse 3, Jesus is sitting on the Mount of Olives. It's not a very long walk, but it does involve quite a steep slope that first descends down into the Kidron Valley, and then ascends back up onto the Mount of Olives. Depending on where Jesus chose to sit, it could have taken him up to 30 minutes to make the hike. And it is not a stretch to imagine that his chosen spot afforded him a strategic and scenic panorama of the city and temple area. Mark tells us in his Gospel that Jesus was sitting directly "opposite the temple" (Mark 13:3).

Jesus' temple teaching that day turned out to be his last public message in Jerusalem.

UNDER SIEGE

On New Year's Eve 2022, I boarded a flight to Israel for the purpose of doing extensive research on this book. My goal was to explore the very sites described in Matthew 24. To feel the Judean dirt beneath my feet. To breathe the air around Jerusalem. To touch the terrain and fully absorb Jesus' view from the Mount of Olives.

During my solo stay in Jerusalem, I meticulously walked the entire eastern wall of the Temple Mount, an area now designated as a Muslim graveyard. Carefully descending the steep incline leading down into the Kidron Valley, my private guide led me to a grate in the ground. Stooping down, we could see and hear the still-running waters of the brook Kidron. We then took a brief taxi ride to the top of the Mount of Olives. From there, we were afforded an unforgettable panoramic view of Jerusalem and the Temple Mount. The temple area stands as a silent testimony to 4,000 years of history. For a Christian, standing at this site makes for an unforgettable holy moment. Afterward, we walked down the narrow street leading to the Garden of Gethsemane. The grade was so steep that even slow-moving cars were screeching down the hill, staccato style. One can only imagine Jesus' fatigue upon reaching his desired spot somewhere up on the mountain. And it's no surprise he sat down upon his arrival.

It was there and then that Jesus' disciples came to him—specifically, Peter, James, John, and Andrew (Mark 13:3). In response to their two original questions, "When will these things happen, and what will be the sign of your coming, and of the end of the age?" (Matthew 24:3), only Luke records the answer to the first one (see Luke 21:20-24). Their initial question was prompted by Jesus' prophecy that "not one stone here will be left upon another, which will not be torn down" (verse 2). Here, Christ predicts not only the coming destruction of Jerusalem, which occurred in AD 70, some 35 years after his death and resurrection, but also the total destruction of the temple itself. Matthew did record a prophecy Christ gave earlier in the day regarding the temple's desolation, but it was given *before* the disciples' admiration of the buildings and Jesus' surprise declaration to them concerning its coming destruction (Matthew 23:38).

The reason the disciples' questions connected the destruction of Jerusalem with the temple was likely due to Zechariah 14:1-11. This passage describes the end of days, when Jerusalem will be attacked by all nations and captured (verses 1-2). But then Messiah will come and destroy the nations, split the Mount of Olives (verses 3-8), and set up his millennial kingdom here upon the earth (verses 9-11). So the disciples knew the correct *chronology* of these events, but were incorrect about the *timing*.

Jerusalem would indeed be destroyed in AD 70 by the Roman general Titus, following a four-year campaign. However, this destruction had also been prophesied by the prophet Daniel 600 years earlier (Daniel 9:26). Having suffered under increasingly oppressive Roman rule for nearly 130 years, tensions finally ignited. When the Roman governor at the time (Gessius Flores) confiscated 17 talents of silver from the temple treasury, the Jews responded by rioting and taking out the small Roman garrison there at Jerusalem. After an initial skirmish and victory by Jewish rebels, Rome responded by sending 60,000 highly trained troops to the area. No Ancient Near Eastern people, group, or nation had ever revolted against the Roman Empire as had the Jews, who were led by militant zealots and sicarii (a group of assassins). By the summer of AD 70, Jerusalem was under full siege by Rome's Tenth Legion, led by Commander Vespasian. But when Vespasian returned to Rome to attend to affairs there, he placed his son Titus in charge. His job was to squelch and crush the rebellion once and for all.

Dr. Randall Price picks up the story from here:

> The Jews celebrated a last Passover with their temple and prepared for the Roman attack. It came days later with a catapult barrage that continued for two months until the Romans finally breached the walls. They set fire to the city, slaughtering every Jew in their wake.
>
> The Jewish defenders held back the Roman assault from the Temple Mount for three weeks. Then, on the ninth of the Jewish month of Av (August), the Romans invaded the temple compound and set fire to it, slaughtering the

priests. The Romans also chopped down the trees in the area to form a huge bonfire around the temple. This caused the moisture in the temple's limestone blocks to expand and blow the stones apart, collapsing the temple in a single day. Josephus records the Romans pillaged the temple, treasury, and storehouses of ritual vessels. The temple lay completely in ruins, with much of its rubble pushed into the Kidron Valley on the eastern side, over the remains of the eastern retaining wall.

The following year, Titus was given a victory procession through the Roman Forum, and the temple vessels were displayed. They were carried by some of the 700 Jewish slaves who were paraded before the emperor Vespasian.[4]

So, Jesus' Temple Mount prophecy came to pass just as predicted. Granted, anyone living in his day could have had a hunch about how the tensions between Rome and the Jews would escalate. But no one could have known that the entire temple itself, along with its surrounding buildings, would be so utterly destroyed and torn down as they were.

Today, when you travel to Jerusalem, you can visit the Temple Mount's Western Wall and see the huge building stones along the bottom of the wall, weighing anywhere from 2 to 15 tons each, piled upon one another in haphazard fashion because they had been pushed over the edge of the Temple Mount platform 2,000 years ago. And there, like an ancient battle memorial, they remain to this day.

CHAPTER 4

HUMANITY
WILL BE DECEIVED

Matthew 24:4-5, 11, 24-26

T ry to imagine what would happen if unexpectedly, hundreds of millions of people suddenly disappeared from the planet. And what if this vast vanishing wasn't due to alien abductions or atmospheric anomalies, but rather, because of a divine intervention prophesied 2,000 years ago? What might be the global fallout from such an occurrence? Without question, the rapture of the church will ignite a comprehensive chaos unprecedented in human history. Fast-forwarding our minds to this future prophetic scenario helps us to envision the seismic shock waves this event will send reverberating all over the world.

Undoubtably, governments and heads of state will be shaken, frantically scrambling to hold their respective nations together in an attempt to keep them from disintegrating into bedlam.

Armed forces across the globe will be catapulted into high-alert status, with potential threats of war likely as rogue regimes look to seize opportunities for invasion or attack.

Cities may be placed under lockdown, sealing in their citizens in place in an effort to stem the tsunami of panic that will grip the world.

Commerce will grind to a screeching halt as stock markets plummet and crash during this hour of unparalleled uncertainty.

News agencies will scramble to create sensational headlines as thousands of media outlets jockey for position to see who can dominate the media market.

Social media influencers will jump online, documenting the moment in real time and engaging untold millions of followers in a worldwide shared moment of crisis.

Schools and universities everywhere will shut their doors, sending students racing home to be with loved ones. The halls of higher learning will echo with silence.

Cell towers will immediately become overwhelmed by the glut of signal traffic suddenly created through massive numbers of calls, texts, pictures, and videos.

Millions of websites will crash due to the extraordinary volume of visitors seeking news, reports, and insights into what has just taken place.

The internet will glow white hot with chatter and posts.

Grocery stores will be inundated with mobs of panic-stricken shoppers overcome by unprecedented dread and terror. Shelves worldwide will be emptied in a matter of hours.

Families will struggle with fear as the reality of missing sons, daughters, brothers, sisters, moms, and dads hits home. Separation anxiety will soar to an all-time high.

Criminals and anarchists will crowd the streets, taking advantage of closed stores and empty shopping centers. Looting, larceny, and lawlessness will explode as hordes of hoodlums flood cities and neighborhoods with robbery, violence, and destruction. Homes emptied of their residents will be invaded by bands of thugs who pillage and plunder for valuables. An epidemic of car thefts will ensue.

Banks and financial institutions will implode due to the economic collapse, and as mortgages default and loans go unpaid, billions of people will be seized by a new frenzy of fear and become emotionally unhinged. Between frantically searching for friends and family members and managing their own collapsing livelihoods, some will resort to suicide while others will seek solace in a mind-numbing haze of alcohol, narcotics, and opioids.

Widespread panic followed by worldwide confusion, universal chaos, and mass hysteria will envelope the globe. Accompanying this will be a lingering dread over other unknown terrors that may lie ahead.

All these scenarios portray only a sampling of what will occur during the days and weeks following the rapture event. And the approximately seven billion people left behind will wonder and ask, "What just happened? Where did the people who disappeared go? What does all this mean? Could *this* be the end of the world?"

A DELUGE OF DECEPTION

At this time in his ministry, Jesus has not yet introduced the prophecy concerning the church's rapture, though he will deliver this promise to his disciples in a little more than 24 hours. Instead, when his closest followers asked him about the sign of his coming and the end of the age, the Lord jumped straight to the time of tribulation. And his very first counsel was to warn that future generation about the immediate rise of false messiahs that will appear during this dark moment in earth's history.

> Jesus answered and said to them, "See to it that no one misleads you. For many will come in My name, saying, 'I am the Christ...'"
>
> Many false prophets will arise and will mislead many...
>
> For false Christs and false prophets will arise and will show great signs and wonders, so as to mislead, if possible, even

the elect. Behold, I have told you in advance. So if they say to you, "Behold, He is in the wilderness," do not go out, or, "Behold, He is in the inner rooms," do not believe them (Matthew 24:4-5, 11, 24-26).

See to it that you are not misled, for many will come in My name, saying, "I am He," and, "The time is near." Do not go after them (Luke 21:8).

Knowing humanity as he did, Jesus was well aware that during any national or international crisis, the first casualty is typically the truth. That's because amid the confusion and absence of discernable, factual explanations, hearsay and rumors often rule the hour and dominate the headlines. But nothing in recorded history will compare to the acute level of disorientation prevalent during Earth's final days. Seeing this as a golden opportunity, counterfeit Christs will pop up across the planet, claiming to be "*the* Christ." They will seize the moment in an attempt to capture and capitalize on their 15 minutes of fame. But they will also seek to captivate the minds and hearts of a panic-stricken populace.

At this time, the world will long for an explanation about this unexpected global emergency and what it signifies. They will seek any sort of answer that gives the reason for this bizarre, unexpected phenomenon. But whenever people long for a sign, they unknowingly make themselves vulnerable and susceptible to deception. And according to Scripture, a great deception will indeed blanket humanity throughout the seven-year tribulation.

We know from the prophet Daniel and the book of Revelation that soon after the rapture a lone figure will rise, positioning himself as the answer to the chaos and confusion that has suddenly gripped the planet. Revelation 6:2 tells us that a rider will appear, mounted on "a white horse, and he who sat on it had a bow; a crown was given to him, and he went out conquering and to conquer."

Some have misidentified this person as Christ himself because he is portrayed as riding a white horse, as Jesus will indeed do according to Revelation 19. However, the contrasts between these two individuals could not be more pronounced. Revelation 6 occurs at the *beginning* of the seven-year tribulation, while Revelation 19 occurs at the *end* of that period. The first rider on a white horse brings peace, while the second one brings wrath. We also know that this time of tribulation will begin with widespread satanic deception, something Christ obviously would not be a part of (2 Thessalonians 2:8-9). Both Daniel 9:27 and Revelation 6:2 indicate that this figure will be an international diplomat and peacemaker. Daniel's prophecy states, "He will make a firm covenant with the many for one week."

The "he" here is the "prince" mentioned in the previous verse, whom the angel Gabriel says will originate in some way from the Roman Empire. Daniel 9:26 predicts the destruction of Jerusalem and the temple, the same destruction Jesus predicted in Matthew 24:2. We know from history that it was the Romans (i.e., the Roman Empire) who destroyed the temple in AD 70. So this coming prince, the same man who will arrive bringing peace at the beginning of the tribulation, will somehow rise out of a revived version of the ancient Roman Empire. This man will be given a crown, which communicates his position of great authority. It is through this platform that he will go out "conquering and to conquer" (Revelation 6:2). Because he is pictured as having a bow but no arrows, his conquest will be a peaceful one. But this, too, is a deception. Paul writes in 2 Thessalonians 2 that this "lawless one" will come "in accord with the activity of Satan, with all power and signs and false wonders" (verses 8-9).

We can deduce from Scripture that the Antichrist will also have a unique connection and relationship with Satan. The word translated "activity" is the Greek word *energeia*, from which we get our English word *energy*. The energy and power to lead that Antichrist exercises will stem directly from the devil himself. He will possess satanic power—or rather, it will possess him. Though some in the Bible are described as being *demon*-possessed, only one other person besides Antichrist is portrayed as actually being indwelt or possessed by Satan himself. John 13:27 records, "After the morsel, Satan then *entered into him*" (Judas Iscariot—cf. Luke 22:3). Judas's desire to betray Jesus, and to deceive the other disciples in the process, was literally put into his heart by the prince of darkness (John 13:2).

Further, Antichrist's satanic activities will include "*all* power and signs and false wonders" (2 Thessalonians 2:9; cf. Matthew 24-24). The Greek words for signs (*semeion*) and wonders (*teras*) are the same words used to describe the miraculous works of Jesus and the apostles (John 2:11; 6:14, 26; Acts 2:22; 6:8). The question then arises: Can Satan perform miraculous deeds on the level of those done by Jesus, Peter, and Paul? Apparently so, as prior to the exodus, Pharaoh's magi were also able to perform such miracles, though there were limits to what they were allowed to do (Exodus 7:8-12, 22; 8:18; 9:11).

The word translated "false" (false wonders) in 2 Thessalonians 2:9 is *pseudos*, meaning "a falsehood or lie." In the context, the word could be interpreted to mean that the signs and wonders performed through "false Christs and false prophets" (Matthew 24:24) are not, in fact, real, but rather, fake, or some sort of elaborate supernatural illusion befitting Satan's deceptive character. While this is conceivable, I take the miracles to be genuine, for the following reasons:

First, there is nothing in the context of these verses that explicitly indicates the miracles are simply some sort of trickery that can be uncovered (like solving a magician's trick).

Second, Jesus and John both refer to these signs and wonders as being "great" (Matthew 24:4; Revelation 13:13), including the ability to call down fire from heaven, as Satan actually did in the book of Job, along with controlling the wind (Job 1:16, 19). Antichrist, via the false prophet, will also miraculously give breath to an image of the beast (Revelation 13:15).

Third, as angelic beings, Satan and his demons are endowed with superhuman abilities, including at times the ability to assume human form (Genesis 6:1-4; 19:1-22). This, too, is beyond a mere illusion.

Fourth, these miracles are 100 percent convincing to "those who dwell on the earth" (Revelation 13:14). This phrase is repeated throughout Revelation and refers to a God-rejecting generation whose doom is ultimately sealed by their refusal to repent of their sins (Revelation 3:10; 6:10; 8:13; 9:20-21; 11:10; 13:8, 14; 17:8).

Surely, if these great miracles were some sort of sophisticated technological trick or sleight of hand, somebody out of billions left behind would figure it out. But they do not. There are no secular skeptics in Satan's end-times domain. Rather, they *all* (except for those Tribulation Jews and Gentiles who trust in Jesus) end up believing and worshipping the beast (Revelation 13:12). In fact, so persuasive and authentic are these wonders that Jesus says they could even mislead God's elect, if that were actually possible (Matthew 24:24).

And as we will see in chapter 9 of this book, Satan is saving his greatest miracle of all for the midpoint of the tribulation. But if these wonders are indeed real, in what sense are they also "false," as Paul states in 2 Thessalonians 2:9? Rather than false being a description regarding the *nature* of these miracles, I interpret the word as pointing instead to their *purpose*. In other words, it's not that the miracles themselves are fake, but rather, that they ultimately lead people to be deceived or to arrive at false conclusions. These miracles are inspired by lies and the desire to deceive, and lead to wrong beliefs, choices, and actions. Just as genuine miracles performed by Jesus and the apostles led to belief in the truth and faith in God, so these satanic miracles will lead humanity to untrue conclusions and beliefs. Certainly, these wonders are married to a multitude of other lies and deceptions propagated by Antichrist and the false prophet during the tribulation. As Revelation's last days' narrative unfolds, Satan will be allowed greater latitude to exercise a host of globally convincing, miracle-working wonders.

A FATE WORSE THAN DEATH

But Antichrist's deceptive agenda won't only flourish during humanity's final seven years. As John explained in 1 John 2:18, not only is the coming of the Antichrist certain, but many antichrists had already risen in John's first-century generation. This, the apostle explains, was how his readers could "*know* that it is the last hour." Essentially, the presence of false christs (Antichrist-like figures) is evidence that we are living in the last days.

All this satanic supernatural phenomenon will lead to a "deception of wickedness for those who perish" (2 Thessalonians 2:10). But lest we are tempted to view that end-times generation as victims, Paul lays the blame at the feet of the deceived ones themselves when he explains the reason they were candidates for Satan's deceptive signs and wonders. He says it is "because they did not receive the love of the truth so as to be saved" (verse 10; cf. Romans 1:28). This highlights a sobering spiritual principle of cause and effect. Repeated refusals to receive and believe the truth of God result in an increased vulnerability to lies and deception. Rejecting the Creator naturally leads to both spiritual and moral blindness, as well as futile speculations about life and reality (Romans 1:21), which, in turn, leads to moronic thinking and idolatry (verses 22-23). Eventually, God runs out of patience with those who habitually spurn his truth and offers of salvation. This rejection is precisely what causes them to be open to embracing demonic deception. It is at this point that God initiates his abandonment wrath protocol, delivering these people over to sexual impurity, homosexual deviance, and ultimately, a depraved mind that cannot be changed (Romans 1:24-32). And once this abandonment wrath happens, these individuals have crossed a point of no return. They are officially unable to repent. They cannot be reached or redeemed.

We are seeing this literally "on parade" today through the demonically driven transgender and drag queen movements of the LGBTQ+

crowd, including men who are convinced they are women, and vice versa. But the irony of all this is that none of these sadly deluded souls ever actually changed their biological gender or basic identity. Rather, their Christ-rejecting minds succumbed to devilish delusions. All the culturally deviant influences and false narratives, and the mental confusion and insanity, is rooted in spiritual deception and depravity. And only God's truth and Spirit are powerful enough to open their eyes and set them free from their prison of perversion.

Even the devil himself knows there is no such thing as a transgender, but he'll never tell because the phenomenon is working so well in his favor. Science and Scripture both attest to the fact that no person can change their biological makeup (sex and gender) any more than someone can magically become a frog or a rock simply by identifying as one. Even so, Scripture tells us that such people are on the path to divine abandonment.

However, from an end-times perspective, I believe this final abandonment wrath Paul specifically prophesies in 2 Thessalonians will occur during the second half (final three-and-a-half years) of the seven-year tribulation. He writes, "For this reason God will send upon them a deluding influence so that they will believe what is false, in order that they all may be judged who did not believe the truth, but took pleasure in wickedness" (2 Thessalonians 2:11-12).

Notice here that at some point Satan is no longer the one sending the delusion, but rather, God. The word translated "deluding" is *plane*, which pictures someone who wanders in delusion. They are lost in space, as it were, drifting aimlessly in a galaxy of lies and alternate realities. Because of this, they gladly receive Antichrist's mark (666), and believe in (put their trust in, rely on) him and all his lies (verse 11). And according to Revelation 14:9-11, every single person who takes the mark of the beast will end up in the lake of fire.

Every one of them.

Not a single one of these souls will repent, for they will have been divinely delivered over to the delusion by a righteous Creator whose patience has officially run its course. No sadder spiritual epitaph could be written:

ABANDONED BY GOD
BECAUSE OF UNBELIEF

This decision to reject the true Christ and receive the counterfeit messiah is also part of God's justification for judging them later at the Great White Throne judgment (2 Thessalonians 2:12; Revelation 20:11-15).

Presently, Satan's last-days' deception has yet to arrive in full force, though we are rapidly racing toward it. His treachery and lies are now surging, permeating both the airwaves *and* brain waves on planet Earth. The continued moral descent into deviance and delusion is but the tip of the iceberg, or perhaps the tip of the spear in Satan's attack on Christ and his truth. As we continue sliding toward Sodom, the devil's agenda to deny and discredit the Creator's truth and existence appears to be working. He isn't called the god of this world, the ruler of this world, and the prince of the power of the air for nothing (2 Corinthians 4:4; John 12:31; Ephesians 2:2).

Meanwhile, back on the Mount of Olives, Jesus is just getting started as he presents his prophecies concerning the last days. Yes, false Christs and world peace will accompany the coming global deception.

But that peace won't last long.

CHAPTER 5

WARS WILL
BE FOUGHT

Matthew 24:6-8

I t has been calculated that over the last 3,400 years, there have only been 268 years during which the world was without war and entirely at peace.[1] That's just 8 percent of recorded history. Some estimate that up to 1 billion people have been killed in earth's wars. World War 1 claimed upward of 40 million dead, with about half of that number due to the Spanish flu. World War 2 saw somewhere between 60 to 85 million perish.

Many wars have been fought for economic or geographical gain. Others were waged for revenge, revolutions, or to defend a country or region. And contrary to common claims, a very small number (7 percent) of the 1,763 recorded wars were fought on "religious grounds."[2] By contrast, atheist leaders like Stalin, Mao, Pol Pot, and Lenin instigated wars that killed 110 million people during the twentieth century alone.[3]

In fact, man's proclivity toward violence traces all the way back to the first child born in the world. After Cain's offering was rejected by God, he wallowed in severe jealousy, anger, and self-pity (Genesis 4:5-6;

1 John 3:12). God's counsel to Cain in Genesis 4:7 was to "do well" (i.e., make an offering in faith—Hebrews 11:4) and to "master" the sin within himself. Instead, Cain simmered in his anger and lured his younger brother to a field, where he violently murdered him (Genesis 4:8).

Some 1,600 years later, mankind had descended into a race of rampant degenerates, to the point where "every intent of the thoughts of his heart was only evil continually" (Genesis 6:5). One way this depravity manifested itself was in unrestrained violence. Though Scripture doesn't give all the specifics, this brutality certainly occurred between individuals, warring tribes, and neighboring nations. In fact, so pervasive was the desire to kill that God twice indicted Noah's generation for causing the earth to be "filled with violence" (verses 11, 13).

The Old Testament itself is replete with accounts of warfare between nations—some warranted, and some evil. And yet even God himself is referred to more than 275 times as the "LORD of *hosts*" (i.e., a mustered army or armed military host). In Exodus 15:3, following God's victory over the Egyptians for Israel's sake, Moses wrote, "The LORD is a warrior; the LORD is His name."

Of course, all of Scripture's God-initiated battles and wars were justified. That's because his character is unchangeably righteous and just (Deuteronomy 32:4). However, for fallen men throughout history, this is not always the case. Aside from clearly defined boundaries between good and evil (for example, the Allies versus Hitler in World War 2), the lines regarding the justness of warfare can easily become blurry in an attempt to justify military engagement and bloodshed.

COMING CONFLICTS

Because humanity is still depraved and sinful, it is fair to assume that conflicts and wars will continue until Christ returns and establishes his millennial kingdom upon Earth. Then, at the close of that

1,000-year reign, one final attempt at war will occur, initiated by Satan, but will immediately be subdued by fire from heaven, devouring the rebels (Revelation 20:7-10). However, prior to this everlasting peace, a perpetuation of warfare is what both Jesus and John prophesy will occur in the last days. Some argue that what Christ had in mind here in Matthew 24 are the great wars of the twentieth century (World War 1, World War 2), due to their "decisive impact on Jewish history."[4] It is argued that because the Olivet Discourse is spoken *to* Jews *about* Jews, there is a direct correlation to Israel regarding the events of the last days (i.e., the twentieth century). This proposition or belief proceeds as follows: World War 1 provided a great motivation for the Zionist movement, and World War 2 helped contribute to the establishment of the state of Israel. Accompanying these prophesied wars were famines, including the great Chinese and Russian famines of 1920–1921, along with pestilence (the Spanish flu that killed 23 million). The growing preponderance of earthquakes is also cited as fulfilling Jesus' prophecies in Matthew 24:4-7.

But even though the reality and impact of these devastating twentieth-century wars, famines, pestilences, and earthquakes cannot be denied, the matter of whether they are actually fulfillments of Jesus' prophecies is hotly debated.

I do agree that the message in Matthew 24 and 25 (the Olivet Discourse) is written to a future Jewish audience, and that these wars Jesus spoke of involve primarily Gentile nations. But the question remains: Where on God's prophetic timeline can we confidently place these warfare prophecies? Do the events of Matthew 24:4-7 occur before the rapture and the seven-year tribulation? Have they already occurred in recent history? Or are they still yet to come?

Studying the context of Jesus' response to his disciples' questions, it seems clear that the generation who will see the abomination of desolation in verse 15 is the same generation he warns about false messiahs (verses 4-5) *and* the future wars (verses 6-7). These same regional or global conflicts are linked to Jesus' words in verse 33: "When you see all these things, recognize that He [the Messiah] is near, right at the door."

Therefore, I interpret the wars and rumors of wars of Matthew 24 to occur within the seven-year tribulation—specifically, during the first three-and-a-half years, and not before. This view fits Revelation's timeline as well. In Revelation 6:3-4, we're told that the rider on the red horse—who is released during the second seal judgment—will "*take peace* from the earth" after the Antichrist grants his peace covenant with Israel (Daniel 9:27). In Revelation 6:4, John states that in these wars, men will "slay one another," and that "a great sword was given to him" (the rider on the red horse). The word translated "slay" (Greek *sphazo*) means "to slaughter or butcher."[5] John is the only New Testament writer who uses this word, and he does so ten times. He utilizes the word to describe everything from the violent, bloody murder of Abel (1 John 3:12) to the murder of the tribulation saints (Revelation 6:9). But mostly, other than one reference to Antichrist's death in Revelation 13:3, John applies this word to the brutal execution of the Lamb of God (Revelation 5:6, 9; 13:8).

The idea is, of course, that this war or these wars will include violent bloodshed. And though since World War 2 the absolute number of war deaths has been steadily declining (as World War 3 has so far been avoided), these prophecies from Jesus and John indicate there will be a dramatic spike in that gruesome statistic in the last days.[6]

According to Revelation 6:8, the first-half tribulation wars will contribute to one-fourth of the world's population being killed. This means that the death toll during the early years of the tribulation will reach astronomical levels. As of February 2024, there are a bit more than eight billion people alive on the planet. If the Revelation 6:8 prophecy were fulfilled today, that would translate to two billion deaths.

This leads to our next question: How and why will these wars be fought?

BOMBING INTO OBLIVION?

Some have speculated that the large number of deaths recorded in Revelation 6:8 could only be explained by nuclear weapons. As of this writing, there are nine countries that verifiably possess nuclear weapons:

Russia—5,977 nuclear weapons

United States—5,428 nuclear weapons

China—350 nuclear weapons

France—290 nuclear weapons

United Kingdom—225 nuclear weapons

Pakistan—165 nuclear weapons

India—160 nuclear weapons

Israel—90 nuclear weapons

North Korea—20 nuclear weapons [7]

Today's nukes, of course, are exponentially more powerful and destructive than any tested or used during or immediately after World War 2. As author David Jeremiah writes, "According to experts, the warheads on just one US nuclear armed submarine have seven times the destructive power of all the bombs dropped during World War Two, including the two atomic bombs dropped on Japan."[8]

Deployed warheads are now strategically aimed at countries like South Korea, Russia, and yes, the United States. They also constantly circle the globe, housed and hidden in submarines running silently beneath the surface of the world's oceans.

Indeed, the combined nuclear weapon capabilities of today's nations contain the ability to destroy the world and its population many times over.

So why haven't we seen a nuclear device launched or detonated in a military attack in nearly 80 years? Certainly this is primarily due to the devastating and deadly domino effect such a strike would cause, as retaliatory attacks would surely ensue. However, we also know from Scripture's prophecies—like the ones found in Revelation—that rival warring countries will never "blow up the earth" through the deployment of nuclear weapons as previously feared. For that to happen, it would essentially circumvent God's pre-scripted end-times narrative. Even so, there will be catastrophic conflicts during the last days that could still potentially involve some nuclear weapons. Jesus himself stated that "unless those days had been cut short, no life would have been saved; but for the sake of the elect those days will be cut short" (Matthew 24:22).

NOTHING TO FEAR

When the Son of Man returns at his second coming, he will prevent the military forces of Antichrist from annihilating the Jewish people, and he will also keep the nations from annihilating one another. And yet, even with this end-times warfare and bloodshed, Jesus' counsel to his followers was not to panic or to be filled with anxiety regarding these wars, but instead, that they should not permit these conflicts to make them anxious: "You will be hearing of wars and rumors of wars. See that you are not frightened, for those things must take place, but that is not yet the end" (Matthew 24:6).

The word translated "frightened" is used only three times in the New Testament, and in each instance, it is in relation to the tribulation period (Matthew 24:6; Mark 13:7; 2 Thessalonians 2:2). The word means "to be unsettled, thrown into confusion, troubled, emotionally upset, or wanting to scream because one is terrified." This is similar to the feeling one gets when a television show is suddenly interrupted for a special news bulletin or breaking news regarding a national tragedy, global catastrophe, or deadly weather event.

So why wouldn't a new follower of Jesus be shaken or terrified when wars and rumors of wars began erupting during the first half of the tribulation? Obviously, fear, uncertainty, and even a sense of panic seem to not only be the natural human response to these things, but even a logical one as well. If wars were to break out across the world now, then life as we know it would be dramatically affected. For example, what if you knew ahead of time that one-fourth of the world's inhabitants would be killed in a soon-to-occur war or series of wars? How do you think that would impact your mental and emotional health? And understandably so.

Yet Jesus nevertheless tells his followers *not* to be frightened. Why? He explains in the second half of the verse: "for those things *must* take place, but that is not yet the end" (Matthew 24:6).

Here, the Lord counteracts fear with knowledge concerning God's *plan* and his *character*. Letting the disciples know that all these horrible things "*must* take place" aligns their minds to God's prophecy concerning his Son's return and his sovereignty in relation to the "end of the age" (verse 3). In other words, God's prophetic chronology for the last days is "necessary" so he can fulfill what he has divinely ordained to come to pass.

And what will that mean for those tribulation believers? It signifies to them, and to us, that our God has everything under his regal control. His purposes not only must be played out on the global stage, but they also cannot and will not be thwarted by man (Job 42:2). This statement of theological truth is designed to give great comfort to the tribulation saints, especially during a time when things on earth will be so out of control. Yes, even during a world war, the Lord is still in charge. There are no maverick molecules in God's universe. He is supremely in charge. And he always will be.

Bible scholar Dr. Thomas Ice writes this about the seal judgment wars:

> Judgment (during the Tribulation) is a necessary part of God's plan because there is evil in the world. Before the

Lord can usher in his Kingdom—because it will be a righteous Kingdom—he must purge evil through judgment. This understandably can be a scary thing if one does not know God and his plan. Grasping the predetermined plan of God is one of the most comforting aspects that prophecy provides for the people of God during a time of global upheaval. Judgment must happen because God is a righteous God who has limits to his patience.[9]

However, the early conflicts Jesus spoke of won't be the only times of war during the seven-year period of God's wrath. Revelation prophesies much more international hostility and bloodshed, both small and large, during that era. These wars and attacks will occur between

- nations (Revelation 6:3-4)
- angels and demons (Revelation 12:7-12)
- demons, Satan, and mankind (Revelation 9:1-12, 13-18)
- Satan and Israel (Revelation 12:13-17)
- Satan against the tribulation saints (Revelation 12:11-12; 13:7)
- Satan and God's two witnesses (Revelation 11:7)
- Jesus and the nations (Revelation 19:19)

And here in the beginning stages of the tribulation, Jesus forewarns, "All these things are merely the beginning of birth pangs" (Matthew 24:8).

What we are experiencing in our world at the time of this writing (the Russia-Ukraine war and the Israel-Gaza war) are not the biblical "birth pangs" Jesus spoke of in Matthew 24:8. Rather, the emerging and converging signs of the times we're witnessing are more like the Braxton-Hicks contractions that precede labor. These pains are experienced by expectant mothers in their second or third trimester. They are sometimes called false labor pains because they feel so much like the real thing.

But though Braxton-Hicks contractions don't signify the actual birthing process, they are significant because (1) they happen only to women who are pregnant, and (2) they precede the eventual, real birth pangs.

It's like the knock on a door before the door opens. One occurs before the other, though the knocking is distinct from the actual act of opening.

PREGNANT PROPHECIES

So, these "prophecies in formation" we're seeing today are previews of the what's next, and they tell us we are in the general season of the Lord's return. We shouldn't mistake the Braxton-Hicks (current events) for the actual birth pangs (prophecies found in Matthew 24). But we can confidently conclude that if we are seeing the one, the other is sure to follow at some point in God's sovereign timing.

And we can be certain of this: Our world is indeed "pregnant" with developing prophecies, and perhaps soon, earth's inhabitants will witness the fulfillment of Jesus' words. However, leading up to those days, we, like those future tribulation saints, can trust in a mighty God who both writes history and oversees its fulfillment.

CHAPTER 6

BELIEVERS
WILL BE DESPISED

Matthew 24:9-10

T he Bible tells us that during the tribulation, a large number of people will turn to Jesus Christ for salvation. As early as the first set of judgments, known as the seal judgments, Scripture describes a multitude of martyrs already in heaven.

> When the Lamb broke the fifth seal, I saw underneath the altar the souls of those who had been slain because of the word of God, and because of the testimony which they had maintained; and they cried out with a loud voice, saying, "How long, O Lord, holy and true, will You refrain from judging and avenging our blood on those who dwell on the earth?" And there was given to each of them a white robe; and they were told that they should rest for a little while longer, until the number of their fellow servants and their brethren who were to be killed even as they had been, would be completed also (Revelation 6:9-11).

These murdered saints are also likely part of the great multitude John sees in heaven standing before the throne and worshipping God in Revelation 7. We learn from that passage that their throng includes representatives "from every nation and all tribes and peoples and tongues" (verse 9). John is informed by one of the heavenly elders, "These are the ones who have come out of the great tribulation, and they have washed their robes and made them white in the blood of the lamb. For this reason, they are before the throne of God" (verse 14).

What can we know about these last-days believers who give their lives for Jesus? How will they come to faith? How will they die? And why?

In the Olivet Discourse, Jesus reveals the first clues for us concerning these mystery martyrs: "They will deliver you to tribulation, and will kill you, and you will be hated by all nations because of My name. At that time many will fall away and will betray one another and hate one another" (Matthew 24:9-10).

Here, Christ uncovers three levels of end-times persecution.

First, he says, "They will deliver you." Second, they will "kill you." And third, "you will be hated by all nations because of My name."

Arrest. Murder. Hatred.

Who is "they" here? The very next verse gives us the answer: "they" are the ones who "fall away" (verse 10). Apparently, concurrent with a latter-days revival involving millions of people, many more will *profess* Christ while not actually *possessing* him in their hearts.

SOWERS, SEEDS, AND SAINTS

In Matthew 13:1-23, Jesus taught the parable of the sower and the soils. In Mark's parallel account, the youngest disciple records that the "sower sows the word" (Mark 4:14). Some of the seed is quickly snatched away by Satan (Matthew 13:19). Other seed falls on rocky ground, and even though it is received with much enthusiasm and joy, this person "has no firm root in himself, but is only temporary, and when affliction or persecution arises because of the word, immediately he falls away" (verse 21). We will take a closer look at these "rocky Christians" in chapter 7 of this book.

The next group are those who dwell among "thorns" (verse 22). They, too, hear the word like the others, but the "worries of the world, and the deceitfulness of riches, and the desires for other things enter in and choke the word, and it becomes unfruitful" (Mark 4:19).

The fourth and final category in Jesus' parable are those who are described as "good soil." This person "hears the word and understands it; who indeed bears fruit and brings forth" (Matthew 13:23).

So according to Jesus, of those who hear the word of truth, only a fraction (25 percent) will prove to be genuinely saved. It is unknown whether this prophesies a specific percentage, or if Christ was communicating that only a small portion of those who hear the word of truth will respond positively and continue on in the faith.

Earlier in his ministry, Jesus declared, "Enter through the narrow gate; for the gate is wide and the way is broad that leads to destruction, and there are many who enter through it. For the gate is small and the way is narrow that leads to life, and there are few who find it" (Matthew 7:13-14).

However, interestingly, the Lord follows up the parable of the sower and the soils with another, this one about wheat and tares. In it, he explains that among the wheat in the field are tares, or weeds (Matthew 13:24-30). These two will grow together and intermingle, all the way up until harvest time (verse 30). When Jesus unpacks this parable, he reveals that the "good seed" (wheat) are the "sons of the kingdom," while the tares are "the sons of the evil one" (verse 38). We know from Matthew 25, at the judgment of the sheep and the goats, God's angels will separate the tares from the wheat, casting the former into the "furnace of fire" (verses 39-42; 25:31-46). We will take a deep dive into this parable in chapter 18.

The bottom-line principle here is that, just like now, during those early days of the tribulation, it will sometimes be difficult to distinguish between real believers and counterfeit Christians. In fact, even some of those false believers themselves apparently won't know that they are not authentic and that their faith isn't real (Matthew 7:21-23).

However, as prophesied in the parable of the sower and the soils, affliction and persecution will arise because of the word (Revelation 6:9), and these people will immediately fall away, denouncing any faith in Jesus Christ. Under intense global peer pressure, they will then eagerly betray and turn in believers whom they may have formerly called brother or sister.

The term *cancel culture* will take on a whole new meaning during the tribulation. Those who persecute believers won't be content to stop at banning or deleting their social media accounts or getting them fired from their jobs. Instead, they will seek to cancel believers' very existence on earth!

The word "deliver" in Matthew 24:9 is also used by Matthew to describe the betrayal of Jesus by Judas Iscariot (Matthew 26:15). We also see the word used in Matthew 4:12 to refer to John the Baptist being arrested and taken into custody.

So, in addition to scores of real conversions during the early days of the tribulation, there will also be false converts. And many of those who deny the faith will deliver believers over to the authorities for arrest, imprisonment, and execution.

CONTEMPT FOR THE CREATOR

From where will this intense persecution originate? Neither Matthew nor Revelation explicitly tells us, but they do provide us with some fairly compelling clues.

First, Jesus prophesies that his future disciples will be "hated by all nations because of My name" (Matthew 24:9; cf. 10:21-22). However, this wouldn't be the last time Christ would warn them about this tribulation-type hatred. Just one day following his Olivet prophecy, Christ gathered his disciples into a large, furnished upper room in Jerusalem (Mark 14:12-15). There, he taught them about the rapture (John 14:1-3), the fact that he alone was the only way to God (verses 4-8), his deity (verses 9-11), the power of prayer (verses 12-14), obedience (verse 15), the coming of the Holy Spirit (verses 16-21), and love for him (verses 22-24), among other topics.

Then they left the upper room and began the walk to the Garden of Gethsemane (verse 31). On the way, Jesus warned his men,

> If the world hates you, you know that it has hated Me before it hated you. If you were of the world, the world would love its own; but because you are not of the world, but I chose you out of the world, because of this the world hates you. Remember the word that I said to you, "A slave is not greater than his master." If they persecuted Me, they will also persecute you; if they kept My word, they will keep yours also. But all these things they will do to you for My name's sake, because they do not know the One who sent me (John 15:18-21).

In short, they will want to kill Christians because they hate God.

Satan and the world have always hated Jesus and those who belong to him (Genesis 3:15). So if we identify ourselves with him and align our beliefs and values with those of his Word, we will find ourselves either quickly or eventually ridiculed, maligned, ostracized, marginalized, demonized, cancelled, mocked, persecuted, hated, and yes, potentially even murdered for our faith.

But do not worry if the world hates you and your beliefs. In a sense, it's not personal. Rather, the way unbelievers respond reveals the inner-heart hatred they have for the God whom you serve.

APOCALYPSE NOW

As I study Matthew 24 and Jesus' description of the tribulation, I see a distinctively Jewish emphasis in the context (cf. Jeremiah 30:7, 11, 23-24; Ezekiel 20:33-44; 22:17-22; Daniel 7:25; 12:1-3; Hosea 5:15; Zephaniah 1:7–2:3). Even so, I do believe this end-times persecution will extend to all who come to faith in Jesus during this time—to both Jewish and Gentile believers (Revelation 6:9-11). So we know that this end-times persecution of tribulation believers will stem from an intense hatred of Jesus and the Father.

But I also see it rooted in the tribulation judgments themselves. When we carefully examine Revelation 6 and the seal judgments, we discover a surprising reality about the unbelievers who will dwell on the earth during that time. Following the sixth seal judgment, which will unleash cataclysmic cosmic disturbances—including a great earthquake, the darkening of the sun, the moon becoming like blood, meteors ripping through Earth's atmosphere, and unprecedented tectonic shifts that alter everything from mountain ranges to islands—the inhabitants of planet Earth will become filled with a level of terror surely not experienced since the floodgates of the heavens and the fountains of the deep opened up against Noah's unrepentant generation (Genesis 7:11).

Doctor Luke records Jesus stating this "prophecy of terror" will fill the hearts of men in those last days (Luke 21:11). And though this end-times persecution apparently will begin before the sixth seal judgment (verse 12), these divine signs of wrath will only exacerbate unbelievers' hatred of Jesus and his followers. In Revelation 6:15-17, we read,

> The kings of the earth and the great men and the great
> men and the commanders and the rich and the strong
> and every slave and free man hid themselves in the caves
> and among the rocks of the mountains; and they said to
> the mountains and to the rocks, "Fall on us and hide us

from the presence of Him who sits on the throne, and
from the wrath of the Lamb; for the great day of their
wrath has come, and who is able to stand?"

Though the Bible doesn't outline for us a precise month-by-month
timeline of the seal judgments, we can be certain of one clear truth:
By the end of the sixth seal judgment, everybody on planet Earth will
know who is responsible for these devastating, deadly occurrences.

By this time, atheism will be gone. Across the globe, not a single
person who once denied God's existence will be found. Gone will be
the conspiracy theorists. Gone will be those who initially blamed the
rapture on aliens or some sort of atmospheric anomaly. No, in that
moment of clarity, the earth will oddly be united under theism—the
belief that there is a supreme divine being, *and* that he is behind all
these judgments. Specifically, unbelievers will reference a sovereign
God on his throne and his dear Son, the Lamb of God. John does
not put words in their mouths or superimpose his thoughts or theology onto humanity. Rather, he gives us a direct quote from earth's
inhabitants. Everyone will recognize that God exists and that he is
the cause of earth's mayhem and their misery. Further, their collective
fear and dread will motivate them to run and hide from the wrath
of God and the Lamb.

This will represent a critical, pivotal moment in history. Consider
what we can know about this scenario, and what people will have
experienced thus far:

1. They will have witnessed the reality and impact of the rapture.

2. They will have watched the Antichrist rise to prominence.

3. They will have suffered through war, famine, and economic
   collapse.

4. They will have seen one-fourth of the world's population perish.

5. They will have somehow survived the first set of God's wrathful judgments.

Now, collectively, these people will not only acknowledge God's existence, but they will also recognize him as the source of all the apocalyptic anomalies they have witnessed. However, they will also fear this vengeful God, which they should, given their unredeemed, condemned condition.

A CRITICAL CROSSROADS

This, for many, will represent a turning point and perhaps a final opportunity to soften their hearts, humble themselves, repent of their sins, and believe in Christ for salvation. It will be a moment of destiny for them. We're not given specifics, but there will be a period of time between the sixth seal judgment and the breaking of the seventh seal, which will inaugurate the trumpet judgments. A pause in the action. A respite. A temporary delay before round two of God's fury descends on the planet. That means there will be time to reflect, reconsider, and repent. For some, this may be when they pivot toward God and beg for his mercy and forgiveness. Others, however, will remain in hiding. Like Adam and Eve, instead of racing toward their creator in contrition and humility, they will run away from him in fear, seeking solace in themselves. This will be a do-or-die moment to either repent or receive more wrath.

And how do we know how critical the hour of decision is here? Because later, John tells us that the vast majority of mankind will eventually transition from *fearing* God to *blaspheming* and *hating* him (Revelation 16:9, 11, 21).

From Revelation's narrative, the message is clear: Turn to God while you still can. While you still fear him. Before your heart is hardened and you grow to hate him.

Sadly, we discover that instead of surrendering to this great, merciful God, most people will stubbornly refuse to repent of their sins (Revelation 9:20-21). They will end up worshipping the Antichrist, even going so far as to publicly declare their allegiance to him through a visible mark prominently displayed on their right hand or their forehead (Revelation 13:11-18).

During the next round of heaven-sent wrath (Revelation 16:1-21), God will unleash his terrible anger on a humanity that has now become officially *unredeemable* (2 Thessalonians 2:10-12; Revelation 14:9-11). And again, their response? They will blaspheme the God of heaven (Revelation 16:9). The Lord will then send a thick darkness upon Antichrist's kingdom (verses 10-11). And once again, people will respond by blaspheming the God of heaven (verse 11).

Finally, the armies of the earth will gather at Armageddon, then come against Jerusalem to once and for all try to *kill God* (Revelation 16:14, 16; 17:14; 19:19). So much for world peace, love, and utopia.

A HEADS UP FOR END-TIMES BELIEVERS

Let's circle back to the beginning of the tribulation for a moment. The tide of public opinion will have already turned against those baby believers who came to Christ just after (and because of) the rapture. These "Jesus people" will quickly discern that to publicly profess Christ will be to put a giant target on their backs—and thus John tells us of Christ followers being murdered in large numbers. From both Jesus' prophecies and Revelation's narrative, we know that mankind is fully aware of who is sending all this tribulation-era pain, suffering, sorrow, and misery. And because unbelievers can't reach heaven and do battle directly with God himself, they will turn their malevolent revenge on those who represent him and his Word here on earth (Revelation 6:9). In other words, they won't be able to destroy God, but they can, and will, brutally slaughter his children.

How will they murder them? We can know for sure that it won't be a quiet, peaceful death, for the word used to describe their martyrdom is "slain" (Revelation 6:9; 18:24). John again uses the Greek word *sphazo*, a term that refers to a bloody slaughter. As we've seen, it's the same word used to describe Cain's murder of Abel (1 John 3:12) and the brutal crucifixion of Christ (Revelation 5:12; 13:8).

Though we aren't told how all of these believers will die, we can assume their arrests, charges, and trials will be swift, with many of them immediately led off to be executed—whether officially by authorities or unofficially by angry mobs. And the preferred method of death? According to Revelation 20:4, *beheading*. The term John uses here refers to having one's head removed with an axe, and it's the only place the word appears in Scripture. *Pelikizo* is a derivative of *pelekus*, the ancient Greek word for battle axe. Properly, it means "to hew or cut with an axe." Granted, this sounds a bit unbelievable, as it is a barbaric method of capital punishment, given that we live in an age of advanced technology and sophistication. However, you may recall that the restraining power and influence of the Holy Spirit (formally expressed through the church) will by this time be gone due to the rapture (2 Thessalonians 2:6-7). Without this restraint, humankind will rid itself of all civility and dignity, devolving into a more tribal-like global culture. This will confirm that all along, it was *Christians* who kept the planet from descending into total madness and depravity as witnessed during the days of Noah (Genesis 6:5-6).

All over the earth, God-hating hordes of humans will be hell-bent on eradicating Christians. Today, believers in 50 to 60 countries are suffering under intense levels of persecution.[1] It is estimated that in 2021, one in seven Christians faced persecution globally.[2] Even in the world of merchandising, we see signs of hatred for Christians and their God. One UK artist, whose other works were prominently displayed in the stores of a certain American retail giant, sold a pin on his website, featuring what he called a "Homophobe Headrest." The pin showed a miniature guillotine, signifying his desire for those who dared to merely disagree with the homosexual and transgender lifestyles.

Another eruption of hatred for Christians occurred when former televangelist Pat Robertson passed away in June 2023. Hate messages proliferated on social media, and crowds already amassed in the streets to celebrate Pride Month cheered and danced upon hearing the announcement of his death.

Though I didn't agree with many of Robertson's views, the fact that so many people across our nation would revel in his death indicates a growing, simmering hatred for all things that have to do with Christ and the Bible.

"They are going to hate you because they hated Me," Jesus reminds us. Don't be surprised. And don't shrink back from expressing both love and truth to a lost, dark, and depraved world.

In spite of this burgeoning animosity, persecution and martyrdom are not headline news. However, during the seven-year tribulation, they will be common, everyday occurrences. Today in America, we risk being ridiculed, hated, and cancelled, but in that future day, believers' heads will be severed from their bodies. This tells us of the level of hatred the world will express toward Jewish and Gentile believers alike. Looking at the world around them, unbelievers will lament the loss of their loved ones through God's divine judgments and they may very well proclaim, "*Your* God did this to us. So now *you* must die!"

Both the context and the grammar of Matthew 24:9 indicate that this intense persecution will take place at the same time as the other early events of the tribulation. Dr. Thomas Ice states that the word translated "then" (*toute*) indicates "not a sequential order of events, but rather a *simultaneous* occurrence."[3]

The fact that "all nations" will hate these Christ followers is further evidence that these events will take place at the end of days, during the time of Revelation's prophecies.

So, what's the forecast for those who embrace the faith during the post-rapture era?

Deliver. Kill. Hate.

Three items that the lost will have on their breakfast, lunch, and dinner menus during the last days.

Those words adequately describe the global attitude toward believers during earth's final seven years, and the seeds of which we're seeing right now.

However, in a plot twist only God himself could write, persecuted Jewish believers in Yeshua will find both help and hope, compliments of their Gentile Christian brothers and sisters (Matthew 25:31-46). Though also threatened with persecution and death, these brave new believers will step up as "heaven's heroes" in a time of crisis and dire need for the Jewish people. With courage and compassion, they will provide clothing, food, comfort, and ministry to the Hebrew followers of Messiah.

And Jesus will be watching.

CHAPTER 7

LOVE WILL
BE SCARCE

Matthew 24:11-13

M any false prophets will arise and will mislead many. Because lawlessness is increased, most people's love will grow cold. But the one who endures to the end, he will be saved" (Matthew 24:11-13).

In the church age, we have seen no shortage of false teachers— from the New Apostolic Reformation (NAR) with their voodoo "grave soaking" practices, to prosperity gospel teachers promoting health and wealth, to universalists and progressive Christians and those who deny the inerrancy of Scripture and embrace apostasy— ours is an era of blatant doctrinal error and departure from biblical orthodoxy. And yet the coming tribulation generation will also see its share of false prophets—not so much within the church (as the bride will have already been raptured), but rather, through false prophets at large who claim to speak and prophesy on behalf of God. Jesus' mention of "prophets" here, and not teachers, indicates that these men are operating almost exclusively within the Jewish community. Keep in mind, the two primary biblical purposes for the seven-year tribulation are to (1) bring judgment on unbelievers, and (2) bring salvation to the Jewish people, or Israel. While we've already seen that a great "come to Jesus" salvation movement will take place among the Gentile nations during the first half of the tribulation, God's primary work will be *in* and *among* the Jewish people. This is the time described in Scripture as Israel's seventieth week (Daniel 9:24, 27), or "the time of Jacob's trouble" (Jeremiah 30:7 NKJV), the culmination of which time "all Israel will be saved" (Romans 11:26).

Think of this for a moment from God's perspective. The Lord had made specific, unconditional promises to the nation Israel, often referred to as covenants (or agreements between two parties). These covenants include:

- The Abrahamic Covenant (Genesis 12:2-3)—an unconditional agreement whereby God obligated himself to make of Abraham a great nation, and that through him all the nations of the earth would be blessed.

- The Davidic Covenant (2 Samuel 7:8-16; 1 Chronicles 17:11-14; 2 Chronicles 6:16)—another unconditional covenant (not dependent on David, but on God) that one of David's descendants (the Messiah) would establish an external kingdom and reign on his throne forever.

- The Land Covenant (Genesis 12:7; 13:14-15; 15:18-21; Deuteronomy 29; 30:1-10)—a covenant whereby God promised eventual possession of the geographical boundaries as outlined in Genesis 15.

Presently, none of these covenant prophecies have been entirely fulfilled. The tribulation (Revelation 6–19) is one of the means to those ends. At the conclusion of the seven years, Jesus Christ will return and inaugurate his 1,000-year millennial reign over the earth, and every one of those ancient promises will see their complete fruition.

With this as a biblical backdrop to God's end-times narrative, the sudden rise of false prophets during the tribulation dovetails seamlessly into that apocalyptic framework. Concurrent with this phenomenon, authentic prophets from God will emerge on the scene as well (more about them in the next chapter).

To counteract these true prophets of God, Satan will send forth his own mouthpieces. Their purpose will not be to point the Jewish people toward the Messiah, but rather, away from him and toward various counterfeit Christs. Their so-called "prophecies" will be fueled by lies, half-truths, and great deception. Some, no doubt, will be self-motivated power brokers seeking fame and a global following. Others, however, will derive their energy and agenda directly from demons and perhaps even the devil himself.

A FAMINE OF LOVE

Jesus now turns his attention toward describing humanity's spiritual condition during the first half of the tribulation: "Because lawlessness is increased, most people's love will grow cold" (Matthew 24:12).

Here, the Lord highlights two dominant characteristics of this end-times generation. First, it is marked by an increase in "lawlessness." The word Jesus uses here is *anomia*, a term that technically means "without law." In the New Testament, the word is typically associated with sin and rebelling against God's righteous standards (Matthew 7:23; Romans 4:7; 6:19; 2 Corinthians 6:14). The word "increased" signifies that this rebellion against God's righteousness will extend to its fullest measure. In other words, it's like a giant dam bursting open and sending a deluge of sin flooding into every corner of the planet.

Now, we have to pause here and ask *why* this happens. Why will the earth be filled with people whose ambition it is to blindly disobey God? Why this end-times explosion of sin? I can think of at least four reasons:

1. The Rapture

As we've seen, upon the departure of Jesus' bride from the earth, the Holy Spirit's restraining influence on sin and evil will be removed (2 Thessalonians 2:6-7). This will be a direct judgment on humanity, serving as a catalyst to chaos. It will result in mankind losing nearly all inhibitions toward a host of sins, including demonic worship, immorality, abuse, thievery, and murder (Revelation 9:20-21). Like the spiritual equivalent of opening jail cells worldwide, mankind will make a riotous run toward what they deem to be "freedom." Unchained from Judeo-Christian values or societal morals and cultural restraints, they will plunge headlong into unchecked evil and wickedness. And with what's left of their consciences on their way to decaying into oblivion, they will both defend and celebrate their depraved attitudes and actions (Romans 1:32). Concerning Noah's generation prior to God's global flood judgment, Moses wrote that the Lord "saw that the wickedness of man was great on the earth, and that every intent of the thoughts of his heart was only evil continually" (Genesis 6:5). This tribulation generation will eerily parallel the one described in Noah's day.

Notice Moses recorded that their sin began as internal motivations, then moved to their thoughts, which, in turn, dominated their minds. Their thoughts led to actions—godless living, corrupt morality, and unrestrained violence (Genesis 6:11-13). In recent years, we have become accustomed to describing both Europe and America as being post-Christian due to the erosion of Judeo-Christian values, as well as the steep slide into gross immorality that has infected our cultures. But during the tribulation, mankind will sink even deeper into an abyss of lawlessness, being then a post-*rapture* generation, and thus officially *pre*-Christian once again.

2. Deception and Delusion

Another reason for this global lawlessness is the consequence of rejecting God prior to the rapture. Jesus has already warned his future disciples that the first sign of the end times will be an explosion of deception. Again, without the bride of Christ present to point humanity back to Scripture and the God-installed conscience that typically holds people back from certain sins, mankind will fall prey to deceptive and sinister beliefs, philosophies, and practices. A global hardening of the heart will take effect. And we're already seeing worldwide evidence of this, though not nearly on the scale that it will be during the tribulation.

This level of spiritual subterfuge will continue to increase as the seven-year period of judgment marches on. At the midpoint mark (three-and-a-half years), a dramatic delusion will be sent, this time not from false Christs or false prophets, but from God himself (2 Thessalonians 2:10-12)! This divinely caused delusion will signify a point of no return with regard to salvation. Their stubborn, callous hearts will gladly choose evil over righteousness, pursue self over salvation, seek pleasure over purity, and serve the devil rather than submitting to the divine Creator (Revelation 9:20-21; 13:3-4, 8, 16-17; 14:9-11; 16:9-11).

3. Antichrist

Satan's secret weapons at the end of days won't be limited to ordinary temptation and the innate sinful desires of the flesh (Mark 7:21-23). Instead, one of those weapons will be embodied and personified in a single man, aptly titled "the man of lawlessness" and "that lawless one" (2 Thessalonians 2:3, 8). Antichrist will epitomize the exultation of self and self-worship. He will single-handedly model for the world what it looks like to mock the God of heaven by blatantly and proudly rejecting him. Scripture tells us that he "opposes and exalts himself above every so-called god or object of worship" (2 Thessalonians 2:4). The apostle John adds this in Revelation 13:5-7:

> There was given to him a mouth speaking arrogant words
> and blasphemies, and authority to act for forty-two months
> was given to him. And he opened his mouth in blasphemies
> against God, to blaspheme His name and His tabernacle,
> that is, those who dwell in heaven.

The verb "to blaspheme" means to hurl "abusive speech or mock."[1] Antichrist's kingdom and administration will be filled with blasphemous policies, laws, and mandates (Revelation 13:1). He himself will speak continual blasphemies against the God of heaven during the final three-and-a-half years of the tribulation (verses 5-6). Specifically, he will mock and malign God's name and God's people who are in heaven (verse 6). He will denigrate and denounce God's character and reputation, essentially attempting to "gaslight" him and smear his name throughout the earth (Daniel 7:25; 11:36). He will no doubt mock and taunt angelic beings (who also dwell in heaven—cf. 2 Peter 2:10; Jude 8).

And finally, Antichrist's blasphemy will also likely be directed toward the raptured bride and recently martyred saints, both of which will be in heaven (1 Thessalonians 4:17; Revelation 4:4, 10; 6:9-11; 19:7-8, 14). As for the new believers who remain on earth, he will declare an unholy war against them (Revelation 13:7). This, too, will be a form of blasphemy (1 Timothy 1:13).

Further, because Antichrist will lead a global coalition of powerful nations, he will wield an international influence never before seen in human history (Revelation 13:1-2; 17:12-13). The world has yet to experience the level of absolute authority this man will possess, an authority bequeathed to him by Satan, who is the god of this world (2 Corinthians 4:4; cf. Luke 4:6; Revelation 13:4-5). He will be hailed as a prince (Daniel 9:26), lauded as an unparalleled peacemaker (verse 27), revered as a king over the earth (Daniel 11:36), respected as a mighty military leader (verses 38-39), and eventually, exalted and worshipped as God himself (verse 36; 2 Thessalonians 2:4; Revelation 13:3-4, 8).

Antichrist's public and persistent blasphemies against the God of Scripture will be applauded and celebrated as good and right (Isaiah 5:20; Daniel 11:36; Revelation 13:5, 8).

4. Judgments from Heaven

A fourth reason the earth will be filled with lawlessness is because of three sets of divine, retributive judgments that will come directly from the Lamb and from him who sits on the throne. These are commonly known as the seal, trumpet, and bowl judgments (Revelation 6:1-17; 8:1–9:19; 16:1-21).

Due to the escalation of deception during this time, people will refuse to repent and surrender to this God of wrath. Instead, they will dig in their heels and display an even greater degree of stubbornness. The direct result of this rebellious choice will be the increase in lawlessness Jesus spoke of in Matthew 24:12. This dramatic spike in sin will become more palatable as people push their own corrupt natures to the limit, reveling in demon and idol worship, thefts, murders, witchcraft, and sexual immorality (Revelation 9:20-21).

Lawlessness.

COLD, COLD HEARTS

Along with this lawlessness, another characteristic of humanity during the end times will be an exaggerated decrease in love. Back in 1965, songwriters Hal David and Burt Bacharach penned what became one of the decade's most memorable songs. Titled "What the World Needs Now Is Love," the song lauded this greatest of all virtues, describing it as something the world needed more of.

The context was that the 1960s saw antiwar protests, the struggle over the civil rights movement, the Manson family murders, and the assassination of three high-profile political figures. In 1967, the Beatles joined in with their own anthem, "All You Need Is Love," which, along with the flower power "Summer of Love" and Woodstock in 1969, preached a combined New-Age narrative of harmony, peace, and goodwill toward one's fellow man.

However, it was not to be.

No historian today would argue that the 1960s brought any sort of lasting peace and love to the world. Sadly, people still refuse to embrace the only real Love who can mend broken hearts, heal relationships, and bring nations together under justice and righteousness. That won't happen until the One who *is* love assumes his throne and reigns supremely in Jerusalem.

That same embodiment of love, seated on the Mount of Olives that Wednesday afternoon as he taught Matthew 24–25, warned his disciples that during the seven-year time of wrath, love itself will sink to an all-time low. And Jesus clearly stated the simple reason for this drought: "because lawlessness is increased, most people's love will grow cold." Put succinctly, lawlessness will lead to a loss of love. This doesn't mean there will be *no* love whatsoever upon the earth, but rather, love will be in very short supply. In a climate marked by wrath raining down from heaven and moral restraints being removed, goodness and kindness will become rare commodities. Paul elaborated on the depraved culture of the last days in his final letter to young pastor Timothy:

> Realize this, that in the last days difficult times will come. For men will be lovers of self, lovers of money, boastful, arrogant, revilers, disobedient to parents, ungrateful, unholy, unloving, irreconcilable, malicious gossips, without self-control, brutal, haters of good, treacherous, reckless, conceited, lovers of pleasure rather than lovers of God, holding to a form of godliness, although they have denied its power; avoid such men as these (2 Timothy 3:1-5).

Consider that the context of Paul's prophecy here applies not only to the world in general, but primarily to those who profess to know God! Concerning the secular world, the apostle portrayed all those those who completely reject the knowledge, truth, grace, and love of God. In his letter to the Romans, Paul wrote,

> Just as they did not see fit to acknowledge God any longer, God gave them over to a depraved mind, to do those things which are not proper, being filled with all unrighteousness, wickedness, greed, evil; full of envy, murder, strife, deceit, malice; they are gossips, slanderers, haters of God, insolent, arrogant, boastful, inventors of evil, disobedient to parents, without understanding, untrustworthy, unloving, unmerciful; and although they know the ordinance of God, that those who practice such things are worthy of death, they not only do the same, but also give hearty approval to those who practice them (Romans 1:28-32).

Sound familiar?

Love in the last days will be as scarce as food in a famine or water in a drought. And the brand of hate prevalent during the tribulation will mirror the animosity many abortion-rights activists exhibit toward pro-life supporters today. Or it will be akin to the vitriolic animosity often seen between those of opposing political parties. The difference is that during the tribulation, the hatred won't be directed only against those who promote decency and traditional virtues. Rather, the hate will overflow and extend to most everyone alive. It won't come from one mean-spirited neighbor or complaining customer. Instead, it will spew forth from the vast majority of humanity.

In such an enmity-filled environment, greed, envy, murder, strife, lies, deception, and anger will fill the air. The atmosphere itself will be hot with hate. There will hardly be anyone a person can trust—not even one's closest family members, as Christ warned in Matthew 10:21: "Brother will betray brother to death, and a father his child; and children will rise up against parents and cause them to be put to death."

Perhaps you're beginning to get a sense of what the quality of life will be like during that awful coming era. It's yet another reason to avoid this awful season of history. Lawlessness. Anarchy. Self-worship. And self-centeredness on a scale none of us have ever seen before. Yes, even the wicked and unsaved will oppose one another. But their deepest hatred will be reserved for those who call Abraham their father and who claim Jesus as their Savior.

As we approach the last days, we are witnessing marked increases in both anti-Semitism and Christian persecution. Yet the hatred and persecution we see now pales in comparison to what will descend upon believers during Daniel's seventieth week.

LASTING IN THE LAST DAYS

In Matthew 24:13, Jesus said, "The one who endures to the end, he will be saved." We can be sure that the spiritual principles Jesus taught earlier in the parable of the sower and the soils are valid today and will still be in effect during this worldwide "hour of testing" (Revelation 3:10). Only a percentage of people will be saved. And we can also anticipate a greater attrition rate among those who initially respond to the gospel. Sadly, there will be some professing Christians who turn on true believers and betray them, contributing to their arrest and even their death. The remainder of these tribulation saints, a much smaller percentage, will endure and bear fruit (Mark 4:20). They will persevere and remain in the faith until death or rescue at the second coming of Christ (Romans 8:30; 12:12; 1 Corinthians 13:7; Philippians 1:6; 2 Timothy 2:10, 12). I believe this principle of endurance is one of the marks of authentic salvation.

That said, I do not interpret Jesus as teaching that particular truth in Matthew 24:13. Even though the teaching about the perseverance of the saints is scriptural, I don't think this is what Jesus was talking about here in this verse.

In Matthew 24:13, the word translated "saved" (Greek *sozo*) is typically understood in a spiritual sense (i.e., to be saved from sin). However, the word does not convey that specific meaning every time it is used in the New Testament. In fact, *sozo* can have several different nuances, depending on the context in which it is used. For example, Matthew himself uses the word to refer to

- physical healing (Matthew 9:21-22)

- deliverance from physical danger (Matthew 8:25; 14:20)

- being saved from death itself (Matthew 27:40-42)

So how is Jesus using the term "saved" in Matthew 24:13? When he speaks to his disciples about enduring to the *end*, contextually, he is speaking of the end of the *tribulation* (Matthew 10:22; 24:13; Mark 13:13; Luke 21:9; see also Revelation 13:10; 14:12).

Dr. Thomas Ice weighs in on this truth:

> Truly, there is a Christian doctrine of endurance taught in the Epistles (Rom. 12:12; 1 Cor. 13:7: 2 Tim. 2:10, 12; Heb. 12:3, 7; James 1:12; 5.11; 1 Peter 2:20). This doctrine teaches that one of the many character qualities that a believer is to have is endurance. Why is this so? It is true because endurance under suffering produces character (Rom. 5:3-4). Yet, none of those references to the Christian doctrine of endurance speaks of "endurance to the end." Instead, passages that speak of enduring to the end all

occur within the same context—the tribulation (Matt. 10:22; 24:13; Mark 13:13; Luke 21:19; Rev. 13:10; 14:12).[2]

In Matthew 24:13, Jesus prophesied that those who endure to the end of the tribulation will be "saved." But saved from what? The answer lies in the context of the passage and of the time of tribulation. We can be certain that Jesus wasn't teaching that spiritual salvation (i.e., entrance into heaven and forgiveness of sins) is somehow earned by persevering to the end. That would contradict both his own words as well as the whole of Scripture regarding how we receive the gift of eternal life. Salvation is not earned by good works (John 1:12-13; Ephesians 2:8-9). Instead, it is a gift that is appropriated through faith in Jesus.

Rather, "saved" here points to *physical* deliverance—specifically, the deliverance of the Jews at the close of the tribulation and the literal return of Jesus Christ at his second coming (Revelation 12:13-17; 13:10; 14:12; cf. Daniel 12:1; Mark 13:13; Luke 21:18-19).

In a time when humanity's love for God will disappear and love for one's fellow man will grow cold, there will yet be a remnant of believers whose love for God will grow *warm*. It is this love, and more importantly God's love for them, that will sustain them with persevering power to last through the most difficult of all days.

And if this is true for them in that day, shouldn't it also motivate us in our day to endure to the end? To persevere and never give up on the God who never gives up on us (Romans 8:28-30; Philippians 1:6)?

Dear saint, as the darkness descends on our age, may we shine as beacons of truth, love, and hope. And may we resolve by God's Spirit to endure for his name's sake!

CHAPTER 8

THE GOSPEL WILL
BE DECLARED

Matthew 24:14

W hile I firmly believe we are living in the last days of the church age and that many of Revelation's realities are rapidly coming into focus, I am also mindful that these prophecies have not yet been fulfilled.

Case in point: After speaking at a prophecy conference in a local church a few years ago, as is my custom, I took time to answer questions anyone might have. With reference to Matthew 24:14, one dear woman asked, "The Bible says the end will come after the gospel has been preached to the whole world. Haven't we surely done that by now, and hasn't that prophecy been fulfilled?"

"Actually, no," I answered. "Anywhere from two to three billion people have yet to hear of Jesus or have any access to the gospel message."

You could almost hear her jaw hit the floor.

Sometimes, because of our sincere desire to hasten the Lord's return, we can tend to move the pin on God's timeline beyond where he has placed it. This is not to say the Lord couldn't return today, because in the New Testament, the rapture is portrayed as being imminent, meaning it could occur at any time.

And though we should have a sense of urgency about our Lord's mandate to make disciples of all the nations, doing this during the church age is *not* a prerequisite for his return.

I went on to explain that Matthew 24:14 does indeed speak of preaching the gospel to the whole world, but that "the end" Jesus refers to is his second coming, which will take place at the end of the tribulation, not the rapture, which will happen before the tribulation.

Christians aren't the only people who wonder if we are living in earth's final hour.

"Is this the end?" is a question being asked by secular scientists paying attention to the ever-changing world around them. As cited in the introduction to this book, just recently, the Bulletin of the Atomic Scientists, an organization formed after the US dropped nuclear bombs on Japan, moved their Doomsday Clock to 90 seconds to midnight. This specifies, in their estimation, that the world and humanity is closer than ever before to global extinction. In other words, even non-Christians believe we are near "the end," though for different reasons than those outlined in the Bible.

CLOSING TIME?

Surely, while sitting on the Mount of Olives that day, Jesus' disciples must have been wondering how near the end was. After hearing him speak of false Christs, wars, famine, earthquakes, persecution, martyrdom, apostasy, hatred, betrayal, lawlessness, and a global shortage of love, they were clueing in that these things must signify the end.

"But not yet," said their Lord. As it turns out, there's much more to come during this time of tribulation. As we will learn, there are far more evils and righteous judgments that will emerge and descend on planet Earth before mankind's final chapter comes to a close. And chief among God's righteous expressions will be the preaching of the gospel.

Christ put it to his men this way: "This gospel of the kingdom shall be preached in the whole world as a testimony to all the nations, and then the end will come" (Matthew 24:14).

Let's now consider the nature of this gospel and how the rest of prophetic scripture tells us it will be spread in those final days.

WHICH GOSPEL?

Using specific and intentional language, Jesus qualified the gospel he spoke of as the "gospel of the *kingdom.*" Why did he describe it this way? After all, isn't the gospel simply the gospel—the good news of salvation through him? Isn't this the same gospel Paul preached, and the one Christians have been proclaiming to the world for the past 2,000 years? Well, yes...and not exactly. Allow me to explain.

Let's first begin with the meaning of the word translated "gospel." It comes from the Greek term *euaggelion,* which means "good news." Good news about what? It's the same good news the shepherds received from the angel on that first Christmas day: "Do not be afraid; for behold, I bring you good news of great joy which will be for all the people; for today in the city of David there has been born for you a Savior, who is Christ the Lord" (Luke 2:10-11).

The good news was that a Savior had come—to save people from their sins, and the penalty that was due them for being sinners (Romans 6:23). Every person is born in sin, which condemns them to a literal, physical, and eternal death sentence (John 3:18, 36).

But the good news is that on the cross, Christ took the penalty of our sin for us. The Father treated the Son as if he *were* sin. Paul, under the divine inspiration of the Holy Spirit, wrote, "He made Him who knew no sin, to be sin on our behalf, so that we might become the righteousness of God in Him" (2 Corinthians 5:21).

Christ died an excruciating death via the brutal means of execution known as crucifixion. What was going on in the invisible realm was another story altogether. Two horrific realities were occurring.

First, God the Father unleashed an eternity's worth of holy fury and wrath upon the Son. No amount of ink or vocabulary will ever be sufficient to describe the level of torment Jesus Christ suffered when he was nailed to that cross. Whatever hell and the lake of fire feels like, that's what he felt. One can only imagine the intensity of God's holy anger and hatred toward sin. And that is what Christ experienced and endured.

But there was a second kind of torment associated with the cross. The penalty of sin is not only physical death and the active wrath of God, but also separation from God. In fact, that is what death is—separation. When a person dies, he or she doesn't cease to exist, but rather, he or she enters eternity—either in heaven with God or in hell without him. When Paul penned Romans 6:23 and said, "The wages of sin is death," he was talking about separation from God and all the good things associated with him.

This is where we must step reverently because there's a bit of a mystery here. Because the essence of the Trinity is unity, it boggles the mind to imagine that the Father could even be separated from the Son. How could there be a divine disruption within the Godhead? And yet in the darkness of that terrible moment on the cross, Jesus cried out, "My God, My God, why have You forsaken Me?" (Matthew 27:46).

And why would Jesus say that? Because God actually forsook him. Somehow, because he was the unique, incarnate God-man, God the Father was justified in removing both his fellowship and his presence from the Son. Do I fully comprehend that reality? No. Is that okay? Yes. For now, we will leave the full explanation of this mind-bending mystery to the Trinity, perhaps to be better explained, understood, and appreciated in heaven and eternity.

Death.

Wrath.

Separation.

That's what Jesus did for *you*...and for *me*. Christ died for sinners (raise your hand if you qualify). And to trust in his incomparable sacrifice is to respond to *the gospel.*

Even so, this is not the complete scope of the meaning of Jesus' words in Matthew 24:14. He did not merely prophesy that the gospel would be preached, but rather, "the gospel of the *kingdom*." But what kingdom was he referring to? And how is it connected to the gospel we all know? Clearly, in context here, this refers to the future kingdom Christ is destined to inherit. It's the same kingdom John prophesied in the seventh trumpet judgment in Revelation 11:15: "The seventh angel sounded; and there were loud voices in heaven, saying, 'The kingdom of the world has become the kingdom of our Lord and of His Christ; and He will reign forever and ever.'"

At first glance, this may seem like a premature declaration because in Revelation 11, the tribulation will still be raging, and the Antichrist will have yet to lose his global rulership. But these words are a *prophetic proclamation.* By this point in the tribulation, the Antichrist will have united the kingdoms (plural) of the world into one kingdom (singular). This will represent the culmination of Satan's long ambition to rule God's world and be worshipped by humanity. You may recall what happened when Satan tempted Jesus: "He led [Jesus] up and showed Him all the kingdoms of the world in a moment of time. And the devil said to Him, 'I will give You all this domain and its glory; *for it has been handed over to me, and I give it to whomever I wish*'" (Luke 4:5-6).

Satan said, "'If You worship before me, it shall all be Yours.' Jesus answered him, 'It is written, "You shall worship the Lord your God and serve Him only"'" (verses 7-8).

Notice that Jesus did not dispute Satan's dominion over the nations or argue the devil's claim. In fact, three times the Lord himself called Satan "the ruler of this [or the] world" (John 12:31; 14:30; 16:11).

Upon careful comparison, we see that Revelation 11:15 and Luke

4:5 reveal a slight but critical distinction. When the devil tempted Jesus, kingdoms (plural) were offered to him. But by the midpoint of the tribulation, they will have become united as *one kingdom* under Satan's Antichrist.

Therefore, the announcement in Revelation 11:15 serves as a prophetic foreshadow concerning Satan, Antichrist, and the false prophet. In other words, by the time of the seventh trumpet judgment, Jesus' future millennial reign is so certain and so guaranteed that those in heaven speak of it as if it's a forgone conclusion. As if it has already occurred. That's how *sure* Bible prophecy is!

So Jesus' reference in Matthew 24:14 to "this gospel of the kingdom" is primarily a proclamation of the truth that he will soon return to rule and reign. And *this* is the gospel that will be preached during the tribulation. What a message of hope this will be to persecuted saints at that time! And it will no doubt constitute a substantive part of what both the 144,000 and the two witnesses will preach. Can you imagine a more irritating and annoying message to Antichrist in his era of power?

"You may be reigning in this brief moment, but Jesus of Nazareth is coming back to take you down and claim his kingdom! He is on his way!"

No wonder Antichrist will seek to kill the two witnesses and the 144,000! During the beast's global reign, God's messengers and ministers will constantly remind the devil of his soon demise by proclaiming this "gospel of the kingdom."

Jesus is returning to take back planet Earth.

Antichrist will fall and be defeated.

Satan's reign will be short and come to an end.

Therefore, believe on the Lord Jesus Christ and be saved. Be on the winning team and the right side of history.

This truth surely enrages Satan. Could it be that this very reminder of his destiny is what motivates him to attempt one final coup in heaven, as stated in Revelation 12:7-9? In fact, the very next verse mentions Jesus' kingdom rule: "Now the salvation, and the power, and the kingdom of our God and the authority of His Christ have come, for the accuser of our brethren has been thrown down, he who accuses them before our God day and night" (verse 10).

So, the gospel heralded during the tribulation period will include not only the urgent invitation to trust in Christ for salvation, but also carry an overt message about Jesus' coming reign. And it will boldly and courageously be announced via the 144,000, the two witnesses, and the tribulation saints.

THE FLYING GOSPEL

There is one more player in this end-times evangelistic campaign we must consider. And he is neither a redeemed man, a chosen group, nor a miracle-working prophet. Rather, he is a specially commissioned angel. Revelation 14:6-7 describes his task and his message:

> I saw another angel flying in midheaven, having an eternal gospel to preach to those who live on the earth, and to every nation and tribe and tongue and people; and he said with a loud voice, "Fear God, and give His glory, because the hour of His judgment has come; worship Him who made the heaven and the earth and seas and springs of water."

Notice that this angel is not stationary, but rather, *flying*. We know that most, if not all, angels possess wings that enable them to fly. We've all seen the rapid speeds at which birds can fly, like the peregrine falcon, which can soar at more than 200 miles per hour. Though angels are likewise created beings, they are also supernatural, and Ezekiel writes that they can travel "like bolts of lightning" (Ezekiel 1:13-14).

John also states that this angel will fly in "midheaven," or in earth's atmosphere, where birds also fly. So this angel will travel very fast—at supersonic speed. If we take Ezekiel's words literally, we could easily conclude that angels possess the ability to travel at speeds up to 270,000 miles per hour. That means an angel could circle the earth in about six minutes.

However, there is scriptural evidence that angels can also appear instantaneously from any distance (Daniel 9:21). In other words, it's likely that speed isn't really an issue here because angels don't seem to be bound by the laws of gravity or the physics of the universe. Again, they are supernatural beings endowed with power by God himself. And this angel will be equal to his global task.

Though we are not told how long this angel will preach his gospel message, there are several insights we can reasonably extract from Revelation 14:6-7:

1. The gospel he preaches is "eternal." In other words, what he says to those on the earth will be just as true in one billion years as it is in the moment he announces it. God and his gospel truth never change.

2. The gospel will be preached to every living human on the planet (i.e., "those who live on the earth, and to every nation and tribe and tongue and people"). Nobody will be left out; everyone will hear the proclamation. An earlier angel, also flying in midheaven, will have delivered a three-pronged announcement of woes upon those who dwell on the earth (Revelation 8:13).

3. Humanity will be called to "fear God, and give Him glory." The angel will essentially announce that Antichrist and Satan are not to be feared or revered—only God. The beast and the devil will be able to destroy a person's body if they

refuse to worship Antichrist, but they will not be able to destroy a person's *soul*. Jesus said that power is reserved for only One, reminding his audience to "fear Him who is able to destroy both soul and body in hell" (Matthew 10:28). Here, fearing and giving glory to God is synonymous with believing in Jesus and submitting one's life to him.

4. By this time, the final hour of God's tribulation judgment will have arrived. Because of the context of this passage, I believe this angel's announcement will come at the midpoint of the tribulation—at the time Antichrist and the false prophet initiate the mark of the beast (666). And "judgment" in Revelation 14:7 could refer to the final series of judgments, the bowl judgments (Revelation 16).

   However, this judgment could also refer to (or include) the great final delusion prophesied concerning those who have stubbornly and repeatedly refused the gospel up to this point. Paul wrote about this in 2 Thessalonians 2:10-12.

   In much the same way that God hardened Pharaoh's defiant heart and "gave over" sexual deviants and God-haters to their depravity and sin in Romans 1, God will abandon all remaining unbelievers who refuse the gospel proclaimed by the flying angel. Beyond this point, there will likely be no turning back, no more chances to turn to God. This will be heaven's official "last call" to be saved, as Satan, the false prophet, and Antichrist will demand total allegiance from everyone (Revelation 13:3-6, 8, 11-18).

5. The flying angel will proclaims God to be the *Creator*. This is significant not only because God has been robbed of this title by the suppression of truth and foolish speculations (Romans 1:18-21), including those about evolution, but also because

it communicates to tribulation-era people that God "made the heaven and the earth and sea and springs of water," and they are his to destroy at his pleasure (Psalm 115:3; Revelation 6:12-14; 8:7-12). The tribulation judgments devastating planet Earth will be one final reminder that "the earth is the LORD's" (Psalm 24:1). It is he—not random elements nor spontaneous evolution—who made the universe, the world, and the people who live in it. It is his planet we inhabit, his food we eat, and his air we breathe.

After this first angel proclaims his thunderous gospel message, another angel will appear and announce the end of Antichrist's world-wide political, economic, and religious kingdom (Revelation 14:8). This will once again reinforce that the "gospel of the kingdom" is rapidly approaching.

Then a third angel will follow and loudly proclaim eternal damnation upon every single person who receives the mark of the best (Revelation 14:9-11).

In summary, the gospel message at the tribulation's midpoint mark is this:

1. Worship God and submit to him as Creator.

2. Antichrist's kingdom is doomed and about to fall.

3. Choose *right now* whom you will follow. If you take the mark of the beast, there will be no turning back. Rejecting this final gospel offer and taking the mark will seal your destiny and reserve your ticket to the eternal lake of fire.

All this angelic activity could occur in a single afternoon, or even before lunchtime on that day.

It is at this time that Jesus' prophecy in Matthew 24:14 will be fulfilled. The gospel will be preached to "the whole world as a testimony to all the nations, and then the end will come."

This begs the question: Why would anyone foolishly wait this late in the game, when his heart and mind are hardened and doomed beyond repentance? If you are reading this, and you are not certain you are saved, I strongly urge you to surrender your heart to this Creator God *right now*. Knowing what we now know about this terrible time of tribulation, why would you hesitate even one more minute to believe on his Son, who suffered for you and paid the penalty for your sin?

Paul expressed this sentiment best, writing to the Corinthians, "[God] says, 'At the acceptable time I listened to you, and on the day of salvation I helped you.' Behold, now is 'the acceptable time,' behold, now is 'the day of salvation'" (2 Corinthians 6:2).

Don't put this off another second, for your eternal destiny depends on it.

Believe in God's gospel of the kingdom!

CHAPTER 9

THE TEMPLE WILL BE DESECRATED

Matthew 24:15-22

June 6, 1944, is not only considered by historians to be a red-letter date in Western civilization, but also a hinge upon which the twentieth century itself swung. For it was on that cool, wind-swept morning that land, air, and sea elements of the Allied Expeditionary Force banded together to execute what became the largest land invasion operation in human history.

This massive military undertaking involved 7,000 ships and landing craft, ferrying and flying 195,000 men from eight nations. Combined, nearly 133,000 soldiers dropped from the sky and charged the beaches of Normandy, France. A few years ago, I traveled to France and walked the beach known as Bloody Omaha, where on that awful, glorious morning some 2,400 men fell, bleeding the beach red. Some never even made it off their landing crafts as they were cut down by German machine gun fire from the cliffs above.

And yet they kept landing and pressing forward, and by day's end, the Normandy coastline was officially secured. Troops then began their push inland to France's interior, and ultimately, to Germany. The end result was that on May 7, 1945, German general Alfred Jodl put his pen to paper, signing an unconditional surrender in the town of Reims, France.

The war was officially over. Evil had been defeated. Europe was liberated, and the world celebrated the long-awaited arrival of peace.

However, were it not for the sacrifices and successes of that June day, victory may not have been secured, and Hitler's tyranny would have marched on to England, and then across the sea to America. It was the day that changed everything.

They called it D-Day.

ANOTHER "DAY OF DAYS"

Since 1944, there have been other pivotal days in history—days that marked generations and etched themselves into the collective consciousness of a people. Jesus reveals for us one such day, which will occur during the future seven-year tribulation. Another "D-Day," one that changes everything, only this time for evil and not good. Jesus calls it the "abomination of desolation" in Matthew 24:15. But this isn't the first time we read about this dreadful day in Scripture. Christ adds that it was previously "spoken of through Daniel the prophet." By the way, in saying this, Jesus validated the accuracy and inerrancy of Daniel's prophecies. And as we turn back nearly 600 years before Christ to that ancient prophecy, we discover that Daniel forecast this day of abomination not once, but *three times*, each time highlighting different nuances of that dreadful moment in time.

These prophecies are found in

- Daniel 9:27
- Daniel 11:31
- Daniel 12:11

There are some who interpret these prophecies as having already

been fulfilled in 167 BC by Antiochus Epiphanes, a Syrian ruler. And
we do know from history that 400 years after Daniel penned these
prophecies, this man, a notorious hater and persecutor of the Jewish people, did indeed invade the temple and slaughter a pig on the
altar, thus desecrating the Holy Place and rendering it unclean for
Jewish sacrifice and worship.[1]

He then proceeded to plunder the temple, robbing it of its silver
and gold vessels. He also slaughtered thousands of men while taking women and children captive. It is recorded that those women
who had circumcised their young boys (and thus identified them as
Jews) were put to death, and Antiochus hung the infants from their
mothers' necks as a public warning to others.[2] So intensely grieved
over this atrocity were God's people that it is said the beauty of Jewish women faded from their faces (1 Maccabees 1:26).

Antiochus Epiphanes, whose name means "God manifest," also
erected a statue of a Greek god in the temple's Holy of Holies, reportedly substituting his own face on the statue (1 Maccabees 1:51, 54).
The Jews would later refer to him as Antiochus *Epimanes*, meaning
"mad one." This abomination of the temple (which caused it to be
desolate) led to a great Jewish rebellion later known as the Maccabean
Revolt. Led by Judas Maccabeus, the Jews successfully cleansed and
restored the temple in 165 BC, and subsequentially defeated Antiochus. I agree that Daniel's prophecy in 11:31 was preliminarily and
partially fulfilled by Antiochus Epiphanes, yet when coupled with
his other prophecies concerning the abomination, I believe we'll see
its final fulfillment during the tribulation.

From Scripture's various descriptions of this future desecration,
we can draw the following conclusions:

*1. The abomination of desolation remains a future event, and thus is
presently an unfulfilled prophecy.*

How do we know this? Because not all of Daniel's divine predictions were fulfilled through Antiochus. Jesus obviously saw this as a yet-unfulfilled prophecy as well. This is what some Bible scholars refer to as a "dual fulfillment prophecy." This means that certain prophecies have both a near and far fulfillment. This could also be referred to as a short-term prophetic fulfillment, with a second fulfillment that is often more complete and literal, as in the case of Daniel's prophecies. Another example of a dual fulfillment prophecy is Joel 2:28-29, which was initially fulfilled in Acts 2:14:18. The rest of Joel's prophecy (Joel 2:30-31; 3:1-2) awaits its fulfillment at Jesus' second coming (Revelation 16:14-16).

2. *The abomination of desolation signifies the breaking of the covenant Antichrist made with the Jewish people.*

This covenant was made three-and-a-half years earlier (see Daniel 9:27, where we read about the "stop to sacrifice" in the temple).

3. *The abomination of desolation is followed by the setting up of an image of Antichrist.*

After the abomination of desolation, an image (perhaps some sort of statue) representing the Antichrist will be set up and worshipped (Daniel 12:11; 2 Thessalonians 2:4; Revelation 13:14-15).

4. *The abomination will occur at the midpoint of the seven-year tribulation.*

Daniel 9:27 tells us "he will make a firm covenant with the many for one week, but in the *middle of the week* he will put a stop to sacrifice and grain offering; and on the wing of abominations will come one who makes desolate, even until a complete destruction, one that is decreed, is poured out on the one who makes desolate."

The "he" in this verse is "the prince who is to come" (Daniel 9:26). The phrase "middle of the week" contextually corresponds to the halfway mark of Daniel's seventieth week (Daniel 9:24-27). And how do we know that Daniel's seventieth week corresponds to the future seven-year tribulation period? Daniel himself helps us out here. Daniel is in Babylon, and the Jews' 70 years of Babylonian captivity is coming to an end. In answer to his prayers, God sends the angel Gabriel to give Daniel "insight with understanding" regarding the future of the Jewish people (Daniel 9:21-22). Here's what Gabriel says:

> Seventy weeks have been decreed for your people and your holy city, to finish the transgression, to make an end of sin, to make atonement for iniquity, to bring in everlasting righteousness, to seal up vision and prophecy and to anoint the most holy place. So you are to know and discern that from the issuing of a decree to restore and rebuild Jerusalem until Messiah the Prince there will be seven weeks and sixty-two weeks; it will be built again, with plaza and moat, even in times of distress. Then after the sixty-two weeks the Messiah will be cut off and have nothing, and the people of the prince who is to come will destroy the city and the sanctuary. And its end will come with a flood; even to the end there will be war; desolations are determined (Daniel 9:24-26).

These verses comprise not only revelation about the return to Jerusalem and the restoration of the Jewish people (verse 24), but also the future of Israel, the final arrival of Messiah and the spiritual restoration of Israel (verses 24-27).

The "weeks" Daniel refers to are weeks of years, with each week representing seven years. This is confirmed in Daniel 9. Daniel had been reading Jeremiah 25:11-12 and 29:10, and had discerned that the captivity would last for 70 years.[3]

Six Prophecies to Be Fulfilled

In Daniel 9:24, Gabriel reveals that a total of "seventy weeks" had been ordained by God "for your people and your holy city." During that total time period (70 x 7 = 490 years), six prophesies would be fulfilled. Three have to do with Messiah's first coming, and three relate to his second coming. They are as follows:

1. To finish the transgression

2. To make an end of sin

3. To make atonement for iniquity

These all point to aspects of Christ's sacrifice on the cross and what he accomplished there. Then come the three that concern God's program and prophecy about the Jewish people, Jerusalem, and the temple:

4. To bring in everlasting righteousness (millennial kingdom)

5. To seal up vision and prophecy

6. To anoint the most holy place

This is an overview explaining these six future realities (from Daniel's perspective). They have to do with important aspects of Messiah's death (numbers 1-3), and Messiah's reign (numbers 4-6). At present, being in the church age, we chronologically sit between numbers three and four.

The Book of "Numbers"

Next, Gabriel gets even more specific concerning these 70 weeks (490 total years). Keep in mind here that the measurement he uses corresponds to the Jewish prophetic (lunar) year of 360 days, not our 365-day solar-year calendar.

This time period (or the prophetic clock) began with the "issuing of a decree to restore and rebuild Jerusalem," which "will be built again, with plaza and moat, even in times of distress" (Daniel 9:25).

Gabriel also reveals that from the issuing of this decree "until Messiah the Prince," there will be "seven weeks and sixty-two weeks." So, let's stop and do the math so far.

7 + 62 = 69 "weeks" (483 years)

Translated into days, is 173,880 days (483 x 360)

We know from Nehemiah that the decree to return with Nehemiah to rebuild Jerusalem occurred in the Jewish month of Nisan (March). Bible scholar Dr. Mark Hitchcock writes,

> The divine prophetic clock for the 70 weeks or 490-year period began ticking on March 5, 444 BC when the Persian King Artexerxes issued a decree allowing the Jews to return, under Nehemiah's leadership, to rebuild the city of Jerusalem (Nehemiah 2:1-8).
>
> From the time the countdown began until the coming of Messiah will be 69 sets of seven (7 + 62), or 483 years. This exact period of time, which is 173,880 days, is the precise number of days that elapsed from March 5, 444 BC until March 30, AD 33, the day Jesus rode into Jerusalem for His triumphal entry (Luke 19:27-44). The precision with which this prophecy was fulfilled is staggering! That's why I call it the greatest prophecy ever given. It stands as a monumental proof of the inspiration of the Bible.[4]

This amazing prophecy was made nearly 600 years before Christ, and yet was accurate to the *day*. But Daniel's prophecy also makes Jesus' epic lament in Luke 19:41-44 leap off the page with new understanding.

> When He approached Jerusalem, He saw the city and wept over it, saying, "If you had known in *this day*, even you,

the things which make for peace! But now they have been hidden from your eyes. For the days will come upon you when your enemies will throw up a barricade against you, and surround you and hem you in on every side, and they will level you to the ground and your children within you, and they will not leave in you one stone upon another, because you did not recognize *the time of your visitation*."

Zechariah 9:9 was also fulfilled on this day:

> Rejoice greatly, O daughter of Zion!
> Shout in triumph, O daughter of Jerusalem!
> Behold, your king is coming to you;
> He is just and endowed with salvation,
> Humble, and mounted on a donkey,
> Even on a colt, the foal of a donkey.

This same day (the tenth of Nisan, or March 30, AD 33) was also the very day the Passover lamb was to be selected (Exodus 12:3).

Now back to Daniel 9:26, where we see the end of the 62 weeks (the previous 7 weeks were the 70 years of Babylonian captivity, so together they add up to 69 weeks). But what about that seventieth week?

Between the sixty-ninth and seventieth weeks there is a pause, or a "prophetic gap." Daniel prophesies in verse 26 that three specific events will occur during this time:

- Messiah will be killed (i.e., "cut off")

- Jerusalem and the temple will be destroyed (this occurred on August 6, AD 70)

- The Jews will suffer from AD 70 until Messiah's return

And who will destroy the temple? History records that it was the Romans. Daniel (via Gabriel) also indicates that Antichrist will be identified in his origin with the Roman people or its empire. This is one reason why many believe Antichrist will be of Gentile descent, and not Jewish or Arab (Muslim).

Between Daniel 9:26-27, we encounter another time gap of undetermined length. The next prophecy he tells us about is the breaking of Antichrist's covenant with the Jewish people and the abomination of desolation Jesus spoke of in Matthew 24:15. So basically, this gap encompasses from Daniel 9:26-27 to the age in which we are now living (the church age).

The result of this coming abomination is that the "regular sacrifice" will be interrupted and shut down (Daniel 11:31; 12:11). The phrase "regular sacrifice" indicates these Jewish temple rituals will have been going on for some time during the tribulation. We can reasonably assume that they began the moment the temple was rebuilt and dedicated, presumably shortly after the signing of Antichrist's covenant with Israel (Daniel 9:27).

5. The abomination will happen right after Antichrist suffers a fatal head wound and returns from the dead (Revelation 13:3, 12-14)

Scripture indicates there will be a successful assassination attempt on the beast.

Antichrist will suffer a "fatal wound" to the head. And the method of attack? John sees in his vision a "sword" (verse 14). The Greek word here is *machaira*, signifying a short sword or dagger. Though some interpret the word *machaira* symbolically, representing *generic* death (as in Revelation 6:4), I lean toward a literal interpretation, and here's why.

First, there is nothing in the immediate context that indicates we should conclude that Antichrist's death, as described, is anything other than actual. Throughout Revelation, the word for death (*thanatos*) is used to describe literal death. So, it appears as if "sword" means the Antichrist genuinely dies.

Second, it's entirely possible that an actual *sword* may also be used in his assassination. Though certainly innovative technology may play a strategic role in Antichrist's kingdom and Scripture's portrayal of the last days, the Bible also pictures a world that returns to an era of barbarism. For example, we encounter both demons and men riding horses (and not hovercrafts) (Revelation 9:17-18), we witness beheadings with "battle axes" (Greek *pelekizo*), and soldiers equipped with "shields and bucklers, bows and arrows, war clubs and spears" (Ezekiel 39:9). This doesn't sound like a purely futuristic society. In light of these realities, the use of a literal sword here cannot be ruled out.

Third, there are no qualifiers or further explanations, as we see in other places in Revelation, signifying this sword is symbolic and not literal (as in "two horns *like* a lamb…spoke *as* a dragon" (Revelation 13:11). John uses no similes or overt figures of speech here as he does in other places—"a face *like that* of a man" (Revelation 4:7). In fact, John uses the word "like" 22 times in Revelation to communicate symbolic or metaphorical descriptions of the realities he saw. But he doesn't do that when he mentions this sword. Though this is not conclusive proof, considering how literally John portrays the rest of Revelation, I take it he is referring to a real weapon (likely a sword of some type) and a real death.

But regardless of the instrument, it effectually ends the life of the global government's leader. And it is after his death and return from the dead that he enters the rebuilt temple to commit the abomination. That act marks an apocalyptic hinge upon which the tribulation itself swings. Following this headline-making event, everything changes— for Antichrist, the world, humanity, and especially for the Jews.

Though I believe Satan is thoroughly backing and positioning Antichrist during the first three-and-a-half years, the devil has yet to peel the mask off his prophesied prince (Daniel 9:26). In fact, one could almost understand and explain Antichrist's initial rise to prominence and reign in terms of an ambitious, power-seeking diplomat, a man drunk on his own ego, fame, and positioning. A man's own depraved sin nature is enough to produce that kind of geopolitical leader (Jeremiah 17:9; Mark 7:20-23).

The prefix *anti* in Antichrist means "in place of" or "against." It could be argued that during the first three-and-a-half years, he is Antichrist in the sense that he is *in place of* Christ, a counterfeit Christ, or a false Messiah. Though he is full of evil and lawlessness, he arrives on the global scene bringing peace and safety, not maniacal tyranny (Daniel 9:27; 1 Thessalonians 5:3; Revelation 6:1-2). However, the portrait of Antichrist in the second half of the tribulation is almost of another person altogether. It therefore appears that the "midpoint miracle" of his return from the dead is what catapults him from merely enjoying the pinnacle of political power to becoming fully possessed by Satan, believing himself to be God and filled with a furious and murderous hatred for the Jewish people.

6. *The abomination involves the desecration of the Jewish temple's Holy of Holies (2 Thessalonians 2:3-4)*

Paul reminds the Thessalonians of this eschatological truth he had previously taught them:

> Let no one in any way deceive you, for it will not come unless the apostasy comes first, and the man of lawlessness is revealed, the son of destruction, who opposes and exalts himself above every so-called god or object of worship, so that *he takes his seat in the temple of God, displaying himself as being God* (2 Thessalonians 2:3-4).

The phrase "he takes his seat in the temple of God" can *only* refer to the most sacred place in that temple (Greek *naos*). In Matthew

24:15-16, Jesus applies this to the "holy place," which would refer to the Holy of Holies where the ark of the covenant and the mercy seat resided. But why? Why would Antichrist invade the innermost and holiest place in the temple? Because that is where the Old Testament says the presence of God dwelt (Leviticus 16:2; Habakkuk 1:13). Antichrist's entrance behind the veil is also evident in Paul's portrayal of him in 2 Thessalonians 2:4, where he describes Antichrist as the one "who opposes and exalts himself above every so-called god or object of worship." And the specific place one would do that in the Jewish temple is the Holy of Holies.

In doing so, this man of lawlessness will brazenly and blasphemously exalt himself to be above Yahweh. But he won't stop there. With the same breath, he will proclaim himself to be *greater* than the true God. He will assert superiority to Jesus Christ, as well as the false god of Islam (Allah), and the plethora of imaginary deities manufactured by man. This, then, is the religious significance behind the desecration of the temple.

During the tribulation, the Antichrist's relationship to the Jews will shift from protector and provider to persecutor. From a velvet-gloved ally to an iron-fisted enemy.

EVACUATION STRATEGY

Note that Jesus doesn't merely give this prophecy and then casually move on to the next topic. He goes on to provide his future Jewish kinsmen with an exit plan. But what instructions does he give them? And why?

In Revelation 12, John describes what many, including myself, believe to be the account of a future attempted coup by Satan in heaven. This one will take place at the tribulation's midpoint.

We know from Job 1:6-11 that Satan is allowed access to heaven, into the presence of the Lord (verse 12). *When* and *how often* he is allowed this access is not specified in the Bible. However, after this final "war in heaven," Satan and his angels will be thrown down to the earth, as there will "no longer [be] a place found for them in heaven" (Revelation 12:8). Upon his last-ever expulsion from heaven, Satan will re-enter Earth's atmosphere enraged with unimaginable rage ("great wrath"—*megas thymos*, or a passionate fury), "knowing that he has only a short time" (Revelation 12:12).

This "rampage wrath" will be targeted specifically at the Jewish people. A proposed mini-chronology is as follows:

- Start of the seven-year tribulation: Antichrist will rise to power

- Immediately prior to the midpoint mark, Satan will attempt a final attack on heaven

- He will be cast out and down to the earth

- Midpoint of the tribulation: Antichrist will be killed, then rise from the dead (Revelation 13:3, 12, 14)

- Antichrist will enter the Jewish temple, commit the abomination of desolation, and claim to be God (Daniel 9:27; Matthew 24:15-16; 2 Thessalonians 2:4)

- The mark of the beast will be initiated, or 666 (Revelation 13:15-18)

- Antichrist will begin his attempt at a final Jewish holocaust (Revelation 12:13-17)

- Michael the archangel will arrive to stand guard over the remnant of Israel (Daniel 12:1)

- The "great tribulation" will begin at this time (Matthew 24:21; cf. Daniel 12:1)

Because Antichrist and Satan will one day launch a final effort to annihilate every Jew from planet Earth (Revelation 12:13-17), Jesus gives a most sobering warning to those Jews living in Judea, Jerusalem, and the surrounding areas at this time. His divine counsel can be condensed to one word: *Run!*

> When you see the abomination of desolation which was spoken of through Daniel the prophet, standing in the holy place (let the reader understand) then those who are in Judea must flee to the mountains. Whoever is on the housetop must not go down to get things out that are in his house. Whoever is in the field must not turn back to get his cloak. But woe to those who are pregnant and to those who are nursing babies in those days! But pray that your flight will not be in the winter, or on a Sabbath (Matthew 24:15-20).

This will be a global hunt party, and the Jews will be the prey. Among Jesus' instructions are for them to

- "Flee to the mountains" (Matthew 24:16)—Probably Bozrah (Petra, in modern-day Jordan—Micah 2:12; Isaiah 63:1-6; Jeremiah 49:13-14; Daniel 11:41). God will protect a remnant there, comprising one-third of the Jews. For the next three-and-a-half years, while two-thirds of the Jews will perish under Antichrist's relentless pursuit and persecution of them, the one-third who have hidden will be protected (Revelation 12:13-17; cf. Ezekiel 20:38; Zechariah 13:8).

- Don't go home to gather valuables (Matthew 24:17)

- Don't return from the field to grab your coat (verse 18)

- Hope that you are not pregnant or nursing babies (verse

19), which would make your journey to the mountains more difficult—Antichrist's barbarism may do to mothers, babies, and children what Antiochus Epiphanes did earlier in 167 BC

- Pray this doesn't occur during the winter (when it would be difficult to flee) or on the Sabbath (as travel is prohibited by Orthodox Jewish law)

THE WORST OF TIMES

In Matthew 24:21, Jesus designates the latter half of the seven-year period as a "great tribulation" unlike anything the world has ever seen:[5] "Then there will be a great tribulation, such as has not occurred since the beginning of the world until now, nor ever will" (cf. Mark 13:19).

Moses, Jeremiah, and Daniel all made prophecies concerning this time of tribulation (Deuteronomy 4:30; Jeremiah 30:7; Daniel 12:1). Jesus told his disciples that while they were in the world, they would encounter and experience "tribulation" (John 16:33). But both he and the rest of prophetic Scripture make a clear distinction between *general* tribulation (which comes from the world during all ages) and *the* tribulation (which comes from God during one specific seven-year period).

The last half of that time Jesus called the "great tribulation," referring to the time period between the abomination of desolation and his second coming.

So just how bad do things have to become in order for Jesus to add a qualifier ("great") to what will already be a horrific time period? In a word, *bad*.

At the same time God will pour out his last set of judgments on the earth (the bowl judgments—Revelation 16:1-21), Satan will unleash his final set of wrath-filled judgments on the Jewish people—called the "elect" by Jesus in Matthew 24:24, 31.

THE CHOSEN

Christ then goes on to say, in Matthew 24:22, "Unless those days had been cut short, no life would have been saved; but for the sake of the elect those days will be cut short." This seems to allude to what is said in Daniel 12:1:

> Now at that time Michael, the great prince who stands guard over the sons of your people, will arise. And there will be a time of distress such as never occurred since there was a nation until that time; and at that time your people, everyone who is found written in the book, will be rescued.

Going back to Matthew 24:22: Why does Christ promise to "cut short" those days of persecution? And who are the "elect" he refers to?

First, the reason those days will be "cut short" (or not be allowed to continue indefinitely) is specifically "for the sake of the elect." Had those days been allowed to continue, every believer would have remained under perpetual attack and likely lost their lives at the hand of Antichrist and his forces.

Second, concerning the time limit imposed on the tribulation period, Mark points out that it is the Lord himself who will cut short the length of this era (Mark 13:20).

Third, God decided long ago that this relentless persecution would not go on indefinitely. In other words, he pre-set a limit so that more Jews would not be slaughtered (almost like the "mercy rule" used to end ball games so one team doesn't unfairly dominate the other).

Fourth, the context of the Olivet Discourse is decidedly Jewish, so the elect here are most likely believing Jews alive during the tribulation. Keep in mind that the elect of the church age will have already been raptured by this time (Ephesians 1:4; Colossians 3:12; 1 Thessalonians 1:10; 5:9; Titus 2:1; Revelation 3:10). Of course, it's conceivable that Christ may also have in mind here Gentile tribulation believers as well (Revelation 17:4). While the narrative seems to be exclusively Jewish, there is a possibility Jesus could be referring to *all* the elect who live through the tribulation.

Either way, it is for the elects' sake that a predetermined time limit is set by a sovereign God for these 1,260 days, and the tribulation will not last a single second more. There will be no overtime.

During those terrible seven years, billions of people will die from God's wrath, and perhaps hundreds of millions more during the *great* tribulation. Sadly, during this time, a great slaughter of Jews will occur as well (Zechariah 13:8). This is a prime reason why Jeremiah called this the "time of Jacob's trouble" (Jeremiah 30:7).

And while there is a promised rescue coming from heaven, for a while, Israel must be subject to even more deception from Antichrist. During times of international fear and global panic, Satan gleefully ramps up his energy and delusions to offer humanity what it desperately longs for: peace and safety.

CHAPTER 10

THE ANTICHRIST WILL DISPLAY MIRACLES

Matthew 24:23-26

Next, seemingly unexpectedly, Jesus returns to the subject of false Christs and false prophets. Why would he do this when he has already warned the disciples about these last-days' counterfeits earlier in his message (verses 4-5, 11)? Are these the same false Christs he spoke about earlier? Or is this a fresh batch of counterfeit Messiahs? Context is key here. I see three reasons Jesus returns to this particular topic:

1. Because of what has just happened in the prophetic chronology of Matthew 24—namely, the abomination of desolation committed by *the* false Christ (verse 15)

2. Because Jews at that time will be vulnerable and in hiding, and desperately hoping for a Messiah (verse 26)

3. Because the fake prophets and Messiah figures will authenticate themselves with supernatural signs and wonders, making them appear to be genuine (verses 24-25)

THE AGE OF WICKEDNESS AND WONDERS

Ultimately, the energy behind these phony religious personas is the master deceiver, Satan. And keep in mind that he is a supernatural angel. As such, he possesses powers that are far beyond human abilities. Historically, he has utilized this ability to counteract divine miracles, such as those done through Moses and Aaron when they appeared before Pharaoh (Exodus 7:8-10). No doubt the sorcerers mentioned in the New Testament were energized by demonic forces as well (Acts 16:16; 19:19). With no compelling reason to believe otherwise, it's safe to say that the devil and his demons have continued their miracle-working activity for the past 2,000 years, particularly in pagan cultures that practice voodoo worship and manism, or the veneration of ancestors.

Even today, in some Catholic traditions, claims of apparitions of Mary or testimonies regarding bleeding statues are not uncommon. There are also assertions of supernatural activity in everything from Eastern religions to paganism to Islam. Claims of divine deliverance from disease through supposed "faith healers" and even resurrections from the dead are found even within certain Charismatic sects.

We must remind ourselves that Satan loves lacing his miracles with a heavy dose of deception, in at least two ways: (1) Some of his miracles are not supernatural at all, but rather, spiritual illusions. This is because he is the consummate liar (Jesus called him the "father of lies" in John 8:44). And (2) he possesses the power to disguise himself "as an angel of light" (2 Corinthians 11:14). What does that mean? What does it look like? Primarily, it signifies that what he presents to his audience is so much like the real things that virtually no one can tell the difference. That's because the devil is a master forger—so much so that he is received and believed as genuine. His miracles are convincing, and his lies are accepted as truth. Twisting and redefining the truth is also a specialty of his. He possesses the ability to tell a lie and even make it sound *better* than the truth! And our culture is swallowing his wicked deceptions—hook, line, and sinker.

Touché, Satan.

However, the prophet Isaiah's words come to mind here: "Woe to those who call evil good, and good evil; who substitute darkness for light and light for darkness" (Isaiah 5:20).

Substitute. That's an accurate description of how the devil's schemes are marketed and sold. He simply replaces the real thing with a fake, like substituting a diamond ring with one made of cubic zirconia, a crystalline form of zirconium. It is described as a simulant, which is a fancy word for fake or imitation. But only a trained eye can tell the difference. And many people are content to wear the imitation and fool those around them into believing they have the real thing. But while the distinction between diamonds and zirconium amounts to merely a difference in cash, fake truth can fool people into forfeiting a chance at salvation and put them on the road to hell (Proverbs 14:12; Matthew 7:13-23).

Some of Satan's deceptions have long fuses. He patiently promotes them consistently and persistently until they gain mainstream acceptance and momentum. But during the seven-year tribulation, particularly in the second half, the gloves will come off. At this time, he will be allowed to maximize his deceptive miracle-working power and publicly demonstrate "great signs and wonders" that mislead everyone on the planet, with the exception of God's elect (Matthew 24:24).

Paul told the Thessalonians,

> That lawless one will be revealed whom the Lord will slay with the breath of His mouth and bring to an end by the appearance of His coming; that is, the one whose coming is in accord with the activity of Satan, with *all power and false signs and wonders*, and with all the deception of wickedness

for those who perish, because they did not accept the love
of the truth so as to be saved (2 Thessalonians 2:8-10).

The Greek words used to describe "signs and wonders"—*semion*
and *teras* (both here and in Matthew 24)—are the same words used
to describe the miracles of Jesus. This alone doesn't prove that they are
actual miracles, but it does show that they are *perceived* and *believed*
to be real. And we do know that the miracles done through Antichrist
or by his false prophet have as their source the devil himself. Satan
will not leave these miracles to a lesser demon, but instead, will personally authorize and energize them into reality.

And what might some of these signs and wonders be? Fortunately,
Scripture reveals a few of them for us:

Miracle 1—Calling down fire from heaven (Revelation 13:13)
This miracle will be performed by the other beast (Revelation
13:11), also known as the false prophet (Revelation 16:13; 19:19). He
will likely perform this sign to mimic the same miracle done by God's
two witnesses during the tribulation (Revelation 11:5). He will also
demonstrate these miracles "in the presence of the beast" (Revelation
13:14). Though we are not told, it is possible that he also mirrors other
miracles performed by God's two witnesses (Revelation 11:5-6). But
whatever they are, Scripture describes them as "great signs" (Revelation 13:13; cf. Matthew 24:24; 2 Thessalonians 2:9).

Miracle 2—Raising Antichrist from the dead (Revelation 13:3, 12, 14)
We are not told that the false prophet actually performs this miracle,
only that it occurs. Revelation 13:3, 12 says the beast's fatal wound "was
healed" (possibly by either by the false prophet or directly by Satan).

It is conceivable that either some elaborate ritual will be staged
(perhaps at Antichrist's funeral?) or that Antichrist will simply appear
again after being pronounced medically dead. Revelation 13:14 says he

who "had the wound of the sword…[will] *come to life*." But regardless of who does the miracle, the wonder is done, or at least believed so by billions. By the way, God ultimately trumps this miracle by doing the same thing for his two witnesses (Revelation 11:7-13).

This rising from the dead will be Satan's magnus opus—*the* sign that will convince the world that Antichrist is indeed God (2 Thessalonian 2:4).

A hundred years ago, so much of what we now experience in our everyday lives would have been seen as miraculous (smartphones, the internet, space travel). So in one sense, humanity has grown accustomed to wondrous marvels. Few things impress us anymore. We yawn at things our grandparents would've thought impossible. But nothing from the worlds of technology, travel, or science can match the ace miracle Satan has up his sleeve. He is simply waiting for a specific and preplanned moment to play it, and thereby win the worship of planet Earth.

Miracle 3—Bringing the image of the beast to life (Revelation 13:14-15)

On the heels of Antichrist's return from the dead, it only makes sense that a statue or image would be erected in his honor, and set up in the Holy Place (Holy of Holies, Daniel 9:27; Matthew 24:15). World dictators and rulers have been erecting statues of themselves for thousands of years, often requiring homage or even worship of them (cf. Daniel 3:1-6).

The Greek word John uses here is *eikon*, which refers to an exact representation. It's the same word used to describe how Jesus represented the Father (2 Corinthians 4:4; Colossians 1:15). It was also commonly used to describe the image of a face on a coin being in the likeness of the one represented. The word occurs ten times in Revelation, each time referring to this image of the beast.

But the miracle here is not the image itself, but in the false prophet's ability to make it *come to life*. He will make an inanimate object (likely a statue) breathe and speak. In other words, it will come to life.

Scholar Buist Fanning writes,

> This cannot be explained by Antichrist because it is clearly understood to be a supernatural act. In the Greco-Roman world, people commonly understood images of the gods to be inhabited by the deities themselves rather than as simply inanimate statues and sometimes it was claimed that they pronounced oracles.[1]

And what might this living statue say? Revelation 13:15 indicates those who dwell on the earth will be told to "worship the image of the beast" or be killed. Therefore, to worship the image of the beast is to worship the beast himself. Satan did this with the statue of Nebuchadnezzar as well (Daniel 3:1-6). Concurrent with the placement of Antichrist's image in the temple, the false prophet will also enact and enforce the mark of the beast, or 666 (Revelation 13:16-17).

So far gone will humanity be at this point that even God will abandon them, sending a deluding influence that further hardens people's hearts so that they believe what is false (2 Thessalonians 2:10-12). This will permanently seal their judgment.

So during the tribulation, Antichrist will deceive people through convincing signs and wonders. And he will lead a system of global government prior to his assassination. Daniel foretold of this one-world government in Daniel 2:31-45; 7. His ancient prophecies, proclaimed some 600 years before Christ, parallel the vision given to John in Revelation 13:1-2; 17:8-17. This emerging kingdom will be the culmination of seven previous satanic attempts to rule the world and supplant Jesus' rightful claim to kingdom earth (Revelation 11:15; 12:10; 19:6; cf. Luke 4:6).[2]

Daniel 7:24 tells us that during this time, there will be "ten kings." We do not know who they will be—only that they are called "kingdoms" and "horns" in Daniel 2:44 and 7:24. But we do know that a one-world government will form in the last days. We have seen attempts toward unifying the world and its governments all the way back to the tower of Babel (Genesis 11). From the great empires of antiquity (Egypt, Babylon, Assyria, Medo-Persia, Greece, Rome) to more recent efforts (United Nations, European Union, World Economic Forum), the devil has tried to bring about his rule of the entire globe. It's possible that during the tribulation, this end-times government will be divided into ten regions (kingdoms) with one leader overseeing each region, and with Antichrist above them all.

What will precipitate this last-days government? How quickly could it form? And what will Satan's second-half-of-the-tribulation deception look like?

I believe an unprecedented global crisis will precede the formation of this government. Calls for a one-world government gained some traction during the so-called COVID pandemic. The devil knows that a worldwide emergency will be needed because it's the only catalyst powerful enough to persuade nations to lay aside differences and to ally themselves for a common cause. In order for an emergency to qualify, it must meet the following criteria:

1. It must impact all nations. Everyone must somehow be affected by it.

2. It must trigger worldwide health and safety concerns. This will open the door for governments to provide relief, protections, and relative calm.

3. It must somehow create a financial benefit for all nations. Want to know where the power is? Follow the money. Financial gain is always a factor during a crisis. Who will benefit and get rich?

4. It must ignite a global fear that can somehow be leveraged

by the ten kings for control of the masses. The order is crisis, chaos, calm, compliance, control.

5. It must be "demonized" in order to inspire the world to unite against it (i.e., we must all work together to do our part to fight the global threat).

All these criteria were met by the COVID crisis. Currently, global elites and heads of government are attempting to do the same with the climate emergency scare, leveraging fear and guilt to gain control of the masses. But don't rule out the possibility of another pandemic or "mystery disease." After all, those in power found such a crisis useful the first time.

The point is, whether an international emergency is real or simply planned and manufactured, evil individuals in power will attempt to seize greater global control through it.

THE BIG ONE

I believe that prior to the events Jesus mentioned in Matthew 24, the rapture of the church will be *the* event that ignites the ultimate crisis of the ages.

Can you imagine the immediate aftershocks this prophesied phenomenon will cause? Can you visualize the tsunami-like waves of panic and fear engulfing every nation? Think of the opportunities for both thugs and tyrants to pounce upon people's wealth and possessions. The rapture will be followed by the lockdowns of cities, shutdowns of businesses, and meltdowns of individuals. Earth's greatest needs in the days and weeks after the sudden disappearance of hundreds of millions will be for calm, comfort, reassurance, and peace. The rapture will be the golden moment promoters of a global governance system have been waiting for.

And who will be to blame for all the chaos and calamity that suddenly and unexpectedly hits the planet like a giant asteroid? What common enemy will the world rally against? Who will be the villain? The scapegoat? The bad guy in this story?

One word: Christians.

No doubt as the man who will be Antichrist is jockeying and lobbying for his prominent position while coalescing governments into one, the rest of the world will be boiling over in a unified hatred for believers. But there will be one problem: The Christians everyone hates will all be gone. They will have been "caught up" to meet the Lord in the air (1 Thessalonians 4:17). They will have vanished. Disappeared. *Raptured.*

Revelation 6:9-11 indicates that early on, in the weeks and months following the rapture, there will be a great last-days' revival. These converts will be comprised of those who were left behind and who come to faith in Jesus shortly afterward. I believe it is these infant Christians who will bear the brunt of the world's hatred, resulting in their martyrdom. "Those who dwell on the earth" (a phrase repeated throughout Revelation in reference to unbelievers who refuse to repent) will target these baby believers, hunting them down, pouncing upon them, and murdering them. Unable to punish those who were rescued from the "wrath to come" (1 Thessalonians 1:10), these unbelievers will identify and kill those who take the place of their predecessors.

As Revelation 6:12-17 tells us, these rage-filled unbelievers will understand that their sorrows (the initial seal judgments) are being brought to them courtesy of the Christian God. From these verses we can confidently conclude that every man, woman, and child of every background and nation will know with certainty that it is God and his Son Jesus who are responsible for their mental anguish and physical pain.

While we were here, they hated us. But remember that ultimately, it's not us that they hate. The source of our belief system is God and his Word. The reason we refused to cave in to a sinful, secular culture was because of our godly consciences and scriptural principles. Those who rejected the Lord hated him all along (John 15:18-25), and they hate us because we are his ambassadors. So during the tribulation, they will take out their wrath on those who become believers after the rapture. They won't be able to personally retaliate against God for the seal judgments that are being poured out upon them, so they will brutally slaughter all professing Christians who are unwilling to deny him.

Rapidly putting two and two together, even a simpleton will figure out that the disappearance of those hundreds of millions of Christians was due to the rapture.

Generally speaking, from what we read in Revelation 6 and Matthew 24 along with Revelation 12, it appears that while God's wrath is poured out during the tribulation, humanity's anger will be aimed at Christians during the first three-and-a-half years, and the last three-and-a-half years will be reserved for Satan and Antichrist's hatred of the Jews.

FAKE NEWS AND FALSE MESSIAHS...*AGAIN*!

Following the abomination of desolation, the devil will chase down the Jews who have fled to Bozrah, then proceed to launch three coordinated attacks on this remnant as outlined in Revelation 12:13-17.

Perhaps initially, he will attempt to lure them out with reports that their Messiah has come and is waiting for them "in the wilderness," or right outside their hiding place. When this approach fails, he will send out rumors that Messiah is "in the inner rooms," or inside a house (Matthew 24:26).

So the progression Jesus describes in Matthew 24 is this, with the verses noted:

Abomination (15) → Run! (16-20) →
Persecution (21-22) → Deception (23-26)

Christ warns his future disciples that no matter where anyone says he is—whether in public or in private—don't believe them. Why not? Because he's already told them through Matthew 24:29-31, "They will know when I return. It will be unmistakable and unavoidable." (More about that in the next chapter.) These tribulation-era Jews won't need anyone to announce that Jesus has come back. His return will be very obvious. That's why Christ gives them a heads-up not to fall for Antichrist's trap.

A similar satanic deception spread among those in the church at Thessalonica. There were false prophets who claimed the rapture had already occurred (2 Thessalonians 2:1-2). This false report caused Paul to write 2 Thessalonians, as certain ones had crept into the flock with supposedly documented evidence that "the day of the Lord has come" (i.e., the tribulation has arrived—2 Thessalonians 2:2). And if the time of tribulation has arrived, that meant (based on what Paul previously taught them), the rapture of the church had come and gone (1 Thessalonians 1:10; 4:13-18; 5:9).

The apostle told the Thessalonian believers that even if someone claimed to have had a vision (a "spirit"), a word from the Lord (a "message"), or even a document supposedly signed by Paul himself ("a letter as if from us"), *don't believe them* (2 Thessalonians 2:2).

As you might imagine, this surprise news from these false teachers shook the Thessalonians' faith, deeply disturbing them (verse 2). In essence, they were being told they would have to endure God's wrath and his tribulation judgments.

Paul followed up with "Let no one in any way deceive you" (verse 3). Then he proceeded to lay out the correct chronology of end-times events, which are as follows:

Last-days apostasy (2:3) → restrainer removed
(i.e., rapture, 2:6-7) → Antichrist revealed (2:3, 8-9)
→ satanic signs and wonders (2:9-10) → God's
deluding influence/abandonment wrath on unbelievers
(2:11-12; cf. Romans 1:28-32)

In Matthew 24, Jesus gave a similar prophecy, stating a comparable warning about false messengers prior to his second coming. And it's possible that those future Jewish tribulation believers will have come to faith in Messiah through reading both Daniel's prophecies and Jesus' words in Matthew 24–25.

The lesson is clear: Discerning believers, both now and during the coming tribulation, desperately need the kind of biblical discernment that comes only through a healthy diet of Scripture and studying Bible prophecy. Not only will this help tribulation-era believers to recognize Antichrist's lies and deceptions, but it will serve us right now as we identify the pervasive *spirit* of Antichrist in our world today (1 John 2:18; 4:1-4; cf. Ephesians 6:10-11).

And by reading this book, you're doing just that.

CHAPTER 11

THE SON OF MAN WILL DESCEND FROM HEAVEN

Matthew 24:27-30

Jesus of Nazareth is coming back to planet Earth.

He prophesied it. The Bible confirms it. And his resurrection is proof of it.

For who could fulfill such a prophecy unless he was alive, right? In fact, in the New Testament, for each time Jesus' first coming is mentioned, his second coming is referenced *eight more times*! This is yet another clear indication from God that we should be focusing on his future prophetic plan. Yes, the second coming is an event that is 100 percent pre-authenticated and guaranteed to occur.

And here, in his Olivet Discourse, the Lord unpacks that glorious event not only for his first-century disciples, but us as well, and for tribulation-era believers. Remember, Jesus had just warned those future disciples not to believe reports of his supposed return "in the wilderness" or "in the inner rooms" (Matthew 24:26). Now he explains why his followers shouldn't fall for those deceptions: because his return at the close of the tribulation will be the most dramatic, visible, and unmistakable event of all time.

THE GLORY AND THE GORY

First, Jesus tells the disciples his return can be likened to lightning bolt streaking across the sky. Like that unexpected and blinding flash of light, Jesus' return will be sudden, catching his enemies all over the world off-guard and flat-footed. I believe this description also portrays the Shekinah glory of God. At that moment, all eyes will instinctively look up to behold the source of this burst of light. This demonstration of heavenly glory will be unlike anything the world has ever seen. While it's true that "the heavens are telling of this glory of God" (Psalm 19:1), in general revelation, nothing so spectacular has ever been witnessed by mortal man.[1]

Second, Christ refers to himself as the "Son of Man" (Matthew 24:27, 30). This was Jesus' favorite title for himself; he used it 88 times in the New Testament, with 32 instances in the book of Matthew alone.[2] Stephen, at his martyrdom, called Jesus the "Son of Man" (Acts 7:56).

This title speaks to Jesus' unique state as the God-man, who is 100 percent God (John 1:1) and 100 percent man (John 1:14). That the infinite, sovereign God of the universe would humble himself to take on human form, to serve, and to be mercilessly slaughtered by his own creation (Philippians 2:5-11) is a truth beyond our comprehension, yet it is worthy of our serious contemplation and attention.

"Son of Man" is also a prophetic title recorded in Daniel's vision of the future Messiah King who will rule forever (Daniel 7:13-15; Hebrews 2:5-9). Jesus also describes his return to earth as the "*coming* of the Son of Man" (Matthew 24:27). The Greek word *parousia* ("coming") properly means "presence" or "arrival" and is used 24 times in the New Testament. Sometimes it references Christ's first coming or incarnation (2 Peter 1:16), while at other times it points to the rapture (1 Thessalonians 2:19) or the second coming (Matthew 24:27).

Third, Jesus describes his second coming as coinciding with the judgment and destruction of his enemies: "Wherever the corpse is, there the vultures will gather" (Matthew 24:28; cf. Luke 17:37).

This verse harmonizes well with John's description of the carnage at Armageddon in Revelation 19:17-18, 20. When Jesus returns, he will smite those who have assembled against him and his people at Bozrah (where the Jews have taken refuge—Isaiah 63:1-6). There will then be battles at Armageddon and Jerusalem (Zechariah 12:1-3; 14:2; Joel 3:9-17; Revelation 14:14-20; 16:12-16; 19:11-16).[3] The so-called "Battle of Armageddon" will actually encompass a campaign made up of several battles. His return visit to earth will be vastly different from his first. At his incarnation, Jesus brought life. At his second coming, he will bring death. The promise of salvation was given at his first coming, but at Armageddon, judgment will be the central theme. At his first coming, he was a humble servant. But at his second coming, he is the sovereign Lord.

John prophesies that so many will die by Jesus' spoken word ("from His mouth comes a sharp sword") that "all the birds" will be invited to feast on the corpses of "kings...commanders...mighty men...horses...those who sit on them....all men...free men and slaves, and small and great" (Revelation 19:18). No battlefield in history has seen the massacre and bloodshed that Jesus will unleash at "Armageddon." There will be a 200-mile-long trail of blood that, in places, will reach four to six feet deep (Revelation 14:20). The imagery Scripture uses is that of treading or stomping grapes in a winepress, where clusters of grapes are pulverized to produce the juice that is made into wine. Several Old Testament passages portray God's judgment as being like treading out grapes in the winepress (Isaiah 63:2; Lamentations 1:15; Joel 3:13).

WHEN WILL JESUS RETURN?

Jesus leaves no room for doubt or speculation regarding the timing of his physical return to this world. Sitting with his disciples on the Mount of Olives that Wednesday, he reveals to them that his prophetic event will occur "*immediately after* the tribulation of those days" (Matthew 24:29).

The seven-year tribulation will conclude with the seventh bowl judgment (Revelation 16) and the destruction of Antichrist's capital, Babylon (Revelation 16:19; 18). For the beast's global reign, this will be the official "turn out the lights, the party's over" moment. The world's satanic savior will be ousted from office by God himself. And with the devil's political kingdom now fallen, earth's clock will strike midnight, as simultaneously "the sun will be darkened, and the moon will not give its light, and the stars will fall from the sky, and the powers of the heavens will be shaken" (Matthew 24:29).

Concerning this same moment, the prophet Zechariah wrote, "In that day there will be no light; the luminaries will dwindle. For it will be a unique day which is known to the LORD, neither day nor night, but it will come about that at evening time there will be light" (Zechariah 14:6-7).

Interestingly, when Jesus died, a similar darkness fell on the land (Luke 23:44). Now, at his reappearance, there will be a planetary blackout. A pregnant midnight pause will serve as a prelude for what is about to occur. While the world waits in darkness, a billion-plus white stallions will gallop from heaven. Leading this heavenly army will be the Captain of the Lord of hosts, the Lord Jesus Christ himself (Revelation 19:11-16). In triumphant regalia, these horses and their heavenly hooves will gallop earthward, following their Creator and King.

Earlier, Jesus' disciples had asked, "Tell us, when will these things happen, and what will be the sign of Your coming and of the end of the age?" (Matthew 24:3). Here, the Lord finally answers them by saying, "Men, *I* am the sign"—he says, "Then *the* sign of the Son of Man will appear in the sky" (verse 30).

The word "appear" is the same Greek work found in verse 27, where Jesus describes the flashing of lightning. Just as lightning brilliantly illuminates and penetrates the dark clouds of a stormy night sky, so the sudden appearance of the majestic, glorious Christ will burst through the midnight atmosphere over Jerusalem, flash-blinding all who see him. And make no mistake: Nobody will miss this arrival. As John records, "Behold, He is coming with the clouds, and every eye will see Him, even those who pierced Him; and all the tribes of the earth will mourn over Him. So it is to be. Amen" (Revelation 1:7).

Initially quoting Daniel 7:13, John's reference to the "clouds" here may be picturing the glory cloud, or Shekinah glory, an extrabiblical term from a Hebrew word meaning "he caused to dwell" or "dwelling of God's presence." First expressed in the pillar of cloud that led the Israelites after they were delivered from Egypt (Exodus 13:20-22), it's the same glory God showed to Moses (Exodus 33:18-20). This glory presence also dwelt in the tabernacle (literally, the place of dwelling—Exodus 25:8-9; 40:34-35).

The Shekinah glory is what led Israel through the wilderness (Exodus 40:36-38). And when the ark of the covenant was lost, the glory departed from Israel ("Ichabod"—1 Samuel 4:17-22). This glory cloud (God's presence) would depart and reappear in Solomon's temple, depending on Israel's spiritual condition (1 Kings 8:11; 2 Chronicles 7:1; Ezekiel 10:18).

Jesus gave Peter, James, and John a glimpse of that glory at his transfiguration (Matthew 17:5). The clouds that received Christ at his ascension may have been glory clouds as well (Acts 1:9), especially because the angels who accompanying him indicated he would return in "just the same way as you have watched him go into heaven" (Acts 1:11). Psalm 104:3 states that the clouds are God's "chariot."

As church-age believers, we, too, will be "revealed with Him in glory" (Colossians 3:4). That said, Jesus' point in Matthew 24:29-30 is to emphasize the impact his arrival will have on the unbelievers who dwell on the earth at that time. Along with the dimming of the sun and moon, which will affect both sides of the earth, there will also be a great astral phenomenon: "The stars will fall from the sky, and the powers of the heavens will be shaken" (verse 29; cf. Isaiah 13:9-10; Joel 2:31; 3:15).

Concerning the heavens being shaken, John MacArthur writes,

> All the forces of energy, here called powers of the heavens, which hold everything in space constant, will be in dysfunction. The heavenly bodies will careen helter-skelter through space, and all navigation, whether stellar, solar, magnetic, or gyroscopic, will be futile because all stable reference points and uniform natural forces will have ceased to exist or else become unreliable.[4]

Luke adds that around this time grown men, stubborn and hardhearted from having repeatedly rejected the gospel while welcoming the Antichrist's mark, will literally pass out from the terror of seeing Jesus Christ burst through the darkness (Luke 21:25-26). His use of the word "fainting" refers to being so shocked from fear that one stops breathing. It is entirely possible that the mere sight of the glorious, regal, conquering Christ will cause men to literally drop dead from fright and shock.

"OH, NO!" AND "HALLELUJAH"

In that instant, the constants of our universe will be moved out of their places, causing the solar system itself to tremble at the triumphant arrival of the King of kings and Lord of lords.

The terrifying appearance of Jesus will trigger an immediate response in all earth dwellers, filling them with a horrific sense of regret and dread. Earlier, they mourned sorrowfully over the loss of their beloved Babylon, Antichrist's capital (Revelation 18:9). However, now they will mourn differently, with a deep awareness of their own impending doom. Why? As Jesus explains in Matthew 24:30, because "They will *see* the Son of Man coming on the clouds of heaven with power and great glory."

This will be the biggest "Oh, no!" of all time, as people realize that the Jesus who had sent the initial seal judgments at the beginning of the tribulation is the very same One whose children they murdered (Revelation 6:6-9) and whose gospel they repeatedly rejected (Revelation 14:9-11). The Lamb has shown up to bring vengeance through his presence, power, and glory. And the unusual manner of his entrance—riding a white horse of victory followed by billions of angels and redeemed saints also riding white horses—will send untold millions into cardiac arrest (cf. Revelation 19:11-14).

Meanwhile, the Jewish remnant will break into a tearful hallelujah refrain of praise. They have believed on *Yeshua Ha Mashiach* and have called on him to rescue them from Antichrist's attempted holocaust (Psalm 118:2; Zechariah 12:10; Matthew 23:39). And thus, all Israel will be saved (Romans 11:25-26).

THE CONQUERING CHRIST

At this point in the Olivet Discourse, Jesus skips ahead in the narrative for Peter, James, John, and Andrew, and talks about when he will gather the Jewish elect from around the world to Jerusalem. Some 60 years later, Jesus revealed similar information to John in the book of Revelation, giving more detailed information about the same event:

> I saw heaven opened, and behold, a white horse, and He who sat on it is called Faithful and True, and in righteousness He judges and wages war. His eyes are a flame of fire, and on His head are many diadems; and He has a name written on Him which no one knows except Himself. He is clothed with a robe dipped in blood, and

His name is called The Word of God. And the armies which are in heaven, clothed in fine linen, white and clean, were following Him on white horses. From His mouth comes a sharp sword, so that with it He may strike down the nations, and He will rule them with a rod of iron; and He treads the wine press of the fierce wrath of God, the Almighty. And on His robe and on His thigh He has a name written, "KING OF KINGS, AND LORD OF LORDS."

Then I saw an angel standing in the sun, and he cried out with a loud voice, saying to all the birds which fly in midheaven, "Come, assemble for the great supper of God, so that you may eat the flesh of kings and the flesh of commanders and the flesh of mighty men and the flesh of horses and of those who sit on them and the flesh of all men, both free men and slaves, and small and great."

And I saw the beast and the kings of the earth and their armies assembled to make war against Him who sat on the horse and against His army.

And the beast was seized, and with him the false prophet who performed the signs in his presence, by which he deceived those who had received the mark of the beast and those who worshipped his image; these two were thrown alive into the lake of fire which burns with brimstone. And the rest were killed with the sword which came from the mouth of Him who sat on the horse, and all the birds were filled with their flesh (Revelation 19:11-21).

While Jesus refers to himself as the "Son of Man" (Matthew 24:30), John reveals additional names and titles for Christ at his second coming, including:

"Faithful and True" (verse 11)

Jesus is described this way in two other places in Revelation (1:5—"faithful witness"; 3:14—"faithful and true Witness"). Here, he has faithfully returned just as he himself prophesied in Matthew 24:30. Christ's character and identity are inseparably linked to his word (Revelation 21:5; 22:6). If he promises to do something, we can rest assured that he will.

"A name written on Him which no one knows except Himself" (verse 12)

There is no point in even speculating what this secret name might be. John obviously sees it but is unable to comprehend it. This highlights the reality that God possesses secret mysteries that only he knows about (Deuteronomy 29:29). And we have to be okay with that.

"The Word of God" (verse 13)

Christ is the *logos* of God, the visible image of the invisible God (Hebrews 1:1-2). In the Greek language and philosophy of John's day, *logos* referred to a word or expression of thought or reason. To them, it was an impersonal concept. But John uses the word to communicate that Christ is the expression, essence, and representation of God (John 1:1-3, 14).

"KING OF KINGS AND LORD OF LORDS" (verse 16)

A robe drapes across Christ's chest and thigh and is prominent for all to see, serving as a public proclamation of his identity. This title announces him to be the unrivaled, sovereign ruler over every king, lord, commander, dictator, despot, prince, president, premier, oligarch, and head of state. It also serves notice to "those who dwell on the earth" that the man they had so fervently followed and worshipped the past three-and-a-half years was an imposter and deceiver, a pathetic pawn of Satan. Isaiah describes earthly rulers as mere "dust on the scales," "less than nothing and meaningless" (Isaiah 40:15, 17,

23-25). And the conquering Christ will reduce Antichrist to just that—nothingness. The people of Earth fell for a fake. But now it's too late.

It is at Jesus' second coming that we will witness the culmination of ages and the final grand unfolding of God's prophetic plan. The root of Jesse will return to claim what is rightfully his and to inherit the kingdom promised to him by his Father.

Keep in mind the following facts about this glorious kingdom:

- It was originally his at creation (Genesis 1:1)
- It was forfeited through Adam (Genesis 3)
- It was unsuccessfully usurped by the nations in an attempt to establish a one-world government (Genesis 10–11)
- It was promised through Abram (Genesis 12)
- It was prophesied to David (2 Samuel 7:16)
- It was foretold in the Old Testament (Psalm 2; Isaiah 9:6-7)
- It was preached by John the Baptist (Mark 1:14)
- It was offered by Satan (Luke 4:5-8)
- It was presented to the Jews (Matthew 21:43; Mark 1:14-15; Luke 4:43)
- It was proclaimed to Mary (Luke 1:31-33)
- It was announced to the magi (Matthew 2:2)
- It was rejected by Israel (Luke 19:41-42)
- It was anticipated by Joseph of Arimathea (Mark 15:43; Luke 23:51)
- It was expected by the disciples (Acts 1:6)
- It was celebrated by heaven (Revelation 11:15-17; 19:1-6)

- And it will be fulfilled by Jesus' second coming (Zechariah 14:6-11; Revelation 19:16; 20:1-4)

As you can tell, Jesus' second coming—which will mark the close of the tribulation—is a really big deal to God. It's also a major game-changer for planet Earth and all who dwell on it.

Zechariah 14:4 states, "In that day His feet will stand on the Mount of Olives, which is in front of Jerusalem on the east; and the Mount of Olives will be split in its middle from east to west by a very large valley, so that half of the mountain will move toward the north and the other half toward the south."

This will be the most-celebrated, game-changing touchdown in all history. And if you know Jesus, you'll be there to witness it!

I had the privilege of studying at Dallas Theological Seminary for four grueling years while earning a Master of Theology degree. During my time there, I was honored to sit under some of the greatest theologians and Bible teachers of our age—men like John Walvoord, Dwight Pentecost, Stanley Toussaint, Harold Hoehner, and Howard Hendricks.

Among my fondest memories of those days is when, in chapel, we would occasionally stand to sing the seminary hymn, "All Hail the Power of Jesus' Name" (to the tune of what's known as the "Diadem" version). The truth contained in that great poetic refrain penned by Edward Perronet in 1780 never failed to stir my heart. And as voices were raised, so too were my thoughts about Jesus. The hymn raised goosebumps on the back of my neck as we loudly proclaimed,

> All hail the power of Jesus' name!
> Let angels prostrate fall.
> Bring forth the royal diadem,
> and crown him Lord of all.

However, my most cherished recollection of that hymn was at graduation. There, just before the final verse, there was a pause, during which our beloved chaplain announced, "Now, just the voices of the graduating seniors." And with thundering resound, the senior class sang as one:

> O that with yonder sacred throng
> we at His feet may fall,
> we at His feet may fall!
> We'll join the everlasting song,
> and crown Him, crown Him, crown Him, crown Him,
> crown Him, crown Him, crown Him,
> and crown Him Lord of all!

Even today, nearly 40 years later, I can still feel the holy quiver in my throat and recall the tears streaming down my face as I joined my colleagues in heralding that glorious truth for the last time together.

But even that experience pales when compared to the real thing, my friend. One day, perhaps soon, you and I will broadcast that same, glorious reality to the whole universe. Riding in victorious triumph, we will celebrate the long-awaited arrival of King Jesus on this earth.

Jesus will have returned, just like he said he would!

PART 3

WHEN WILL THESE THINGS TAKE PLACE?

CHAPTER 12

THE JEWISH PEOPLE ARE PRESERVED

Matthew 24:31-36

U pon seeing the Son of Man bursting through the velvet clouds, the Jews who have believed in Messiah through the two witnesses and the 144,000 will "look on [Him] whom they have pierced" (Zechariah 12:10; cf. Isaiah 53:5; Revelation 1:7). Keep in mind that both unbelievers and believers will witness the return of Christ because it will be a supernaturally visible event witnessed *globally*.

MORNING AND EVENING

Jesus foretold on the Mount of Olives that all the tribes of the earth will mourn when they see him suddenly appear in the blinding light of the Shekinah glory (Matthew 24:30). Whenever Revelation describes people groups, nations, and races as being "of the earth" or "on the earth," it typically refers to unbelievers (Revelation 3:10; 6:10; 8:13; 11:10; 13:8, 14; 17:8). And we know from Scripture that there is a type of sorrow, regret, and mourning that, while real, nevertheless doesn't lead to repentance and salvation

(2 Corinthians 7:10). There is remorse, but no repentance, due to the hardness of the heart.

Remember Pharaoh? Following the seventh plague (a deluge of hail), Egypt's leader declared to Moses and Aaron, "I have sinned this time; the LORD is the righteous one, and I and my people are the wicked ones" (Exodus 9:27). He experienced emotional remorse and even intellectually acknowledged the righteousness of God. However, Moses saw through to Pharaoh's soul and knew there would be no real follow-through to real repentance (verse 30). Sure enough, as soon as the plague of hail ceased, Pharaoh "sinned again and hardened his heart" (verse 34). And because of this, God himself hardened Pharaoh's heart (verse 35; cf, 10:1, 27; 14:4, 5).

You'll also recall that after Judas betrayed Jesus in the Garden of Gethsemane, and after he saw Jesus condemned by the Jewish religious leaders, he "felt remorse" emotionally. In fact, Judas even attempted to right his wrong by returning the 30 pieces of silver to the chief priest and elders, confessing to them, "I have sinned by betraying innocent blood" (Matthew 27:4). But he confessed his sin only to men and not God, from whom he could have received forgiveness. He applied the penalty for his sin on himself, committing suicide by hanging (Matthew 24:5). This self-punishment did nothing to atone for his sins of perpetual thievery and the betrayal of God's Son (Matthew 26:24; Luke 22:3; John 12:6; 17:12; Acts 1:25).

Similarly, all those alive at the second coming who have rejected Jesus and taken Antichrist's mark will indeed mourn at Jesus' appearance, but with a deep sense of dread concerning their impending damnation. In fact, not a single one of them will repent and be saved (Revelation 14:9-11).

A PRAYER FOR THE AGES

However, there is also a mourning and sorrow that *does* lead to repentance and salvation (2 Corinthians 7:9-10). I believe this is the type of mourning a Jewish remnant will exhibit at this time, as Zechariah prophesied 2,500 years ago:

> I will pour out on the house of David and on the inhabitants of Jerusalem, the Spirit of grace and of supplication, so that they will look on Me whom they have pierced; and they will mourn for Him, as one mourns for an only son, and they will weep bitterly over Him like the bitter weeping over a firstborn (Zechariah 12:10).

Scripture unveils several successive prophesies that will be fulfilled at the revelation of Jesus "in that day," a phrase Zechariah used 16 times in reference to the day of the Lord.

First, God will pour out his Spirit on the Jewish people, bringing "grace" and "supplication." Second, they will see with their own eyes the Messiah they murdered. But in what sense are the Jews culpable for the death of Christ? During the Middle Ages and the dominion of the Catholic Church in Christendom, Jews were unfairly branded as "Christ killers." This led to an ongoing brutal persecution and slaughter of Jews during that time.[1] But in truth, the Jewish people of Jesus' day were not the only ones guilty of his death. Certainly the Roman authorities who condemned him to death were also responsible, along with the soldiers who drove the spikes into his hands and feet, and the one who pierced his side with a spear (John 19:1-2, 17-18, 34).

Ultimately, however, it was *our* sin that nailed him to that roughhewn wooden beam in AD 33. Though it was Jesus' great love for us that led him to the cross and kept him there, it is you and I who bear the actual guilt of his death. Had we not been sinners, he never would have had to die as a sin sacrifice in our place (Romans 5:8).

But during this future moment in time as described by the prophet Zechariah, God will not apply his redemptive salvation toward the world, the armies gathered at Armageddon, or any remaining

666-branded unbelievers. No. Instead, Jesus will direct the eyes and hearts of every Jew to "look on Me whom they have pierced." In this instance, he will specifically focus his heart on Israel. And how will they respond to the sight of their once-rejected Messiah? Again, "they will *mourn* for Him, as one mourns for an only son, and they will weep bitterly over Him like the bitter weeping over a first born" (Zechariah 12:10). The prophet then adds, "In that day there will be great mourning in Jerusalem" (Zechariah 12:11).

This is the kind of mourning that leads to repentance. In this case, the repentance will be both national and individual (verses 11-13). Just two days before his prophetic sermon on the Mount of Olives, Jesus had lamented,

> Jerusalem, Jerusalem, who kills the prophets and stones those who have been sent to her! How often I wanted to gather your children together, the way a hen gathers her chicks under her wings, and you were unwilling. Behold, your house is being left to you desolate! For I say to you, from now on you will not see Me until you say, "Blessed is He who comes in the name of the Lord!" (Matthew 23:37-39).

Upon Israel's rejection of Christ as their Messiah, Jesus prophesied that the people would not see him again (following his ascension) until they welcomed him at his second coming. This will mark the moment when the "times of the Gentiles" will officially come to an end (Luke 21:24). As Paul wrote:

> I do not want you, brethren, to be uninformed of this mystery—so that you will not be wise in your own estimation—that a partial hardening has happened to Israel *until the fullness of the Gentiles has come in; and so all Israel will be saved*; just as it is written, "The Deliverer

will come from Zion, He will remove ungodliness from Jacob." "This is My covenant with them, when I take away their sins" (Romans 11:25-27).

Christ's return will bring about the prophesied salvation of national Israel. All told, one-third of the Jews left alive at that time will be saved. Two-thirds will have perished during the tribulation, with the rest surviving to witness Messiah's return (Zechariah 13:8-9; cf. Ezekiel 20:33-38).

In desperation, this remnant will call upon the Lord to save them from Antichrist and his forces. At the same time that this ancient prophecy of national repentance gives us a glimpse into the heart of God for his covenant people, it also provides us a peek into the dark mind of Satan during the tribulation. Think of it: As long as there are Jews still alive, they can call upon their Messiah for salvation. But if Satan (through Antichrist and his forces) can somehow annihilate the Hebrew race once and for all, there will be no Jews to save, and thus (theoretically) no reason for the Messiah to appear from heaven and bring them to repentance (or mourning). And if Jesus doesn't return, Antichrist and Satan can continue to rule the earth and be worshipped in perpetuity. This explains yet another reason why the devil will be filled with "great wrath" during the second half of the tribulation (Revelation 12:12)—he must get rid of all Jews!

COME TOGETHER

In Matthew 24:31, Jesus says it is at this time that "He will send forth His angels with a great trumpet and they will gather together His elect from the four winds, from one end of the sky to the other."

Christ's first-century desire to gather Israel's children together will finally be realized at this time (Matthew 23:37). Israel is first prophesied as being gathered from the nations back to the land (Ezekiel

36–37), albeit in unbelief. This promise is both a *fulfilled* (1948, when Israel became a nation again) and *ongoing* prophecy, as virtually every day, Jews are returning to the holy land from around the world. In the prophecy concerning this regathering, Ezekiel 37:6-10 predicted that Jews would return to their promised land in stages. In other words, it would be a *process*.

In Ezekiel's vision of the valley of dry bones, first, there was just bones. Then sinews (tendons, ligaments). Then flesh and skin appear. Last, the breath of life is breathed into the bodies (Ezekiel 37:1-10).

And this is precisely how the Jews have returned—in stages. Hebrew scholar Michael Rydelnik writes,

> There were five separate aliyot (immigration waves) from 1881 to 1939, returning Jewish people from Europe to the Promised Land. After Israel's birth in 1948, an estimated one million European Jewish survivors of the Holocaust came to Israel, followed by a majority of the 800,000 Jewish people driven from their homes in Arab countries. More recently, 1.5 million Jewish people fled the former Soviet Union and immigrated to Israel. These immigration waves show how the Jewish people have returned in stages. The body without breath represents unbelieving Israel, restored but not yet regenerated. Finally, according to this passage, God breathes life into these bodies, representing the day when all Israel turns to the Messiah.[2]

As if guided by an unseen hand, the Jewish people are regathering to the land. And Bible prophecy is being realized.

HEAVENLY BRASS

In Matthew 24:31, Jesus quotes Isaiah 27:12-13. In both passages, a gathering is predicted. Both prophesy of a trumpet, and both portray all Jews coming to Jerusalem to meet the Lord. So there is an obvious prophetic connection between the passages. Both mention a "great trumpet," and both refer to the same event.

Some people today seek to find a parallel between the Jewish Feast of Trumpets and the rapture, which also features a last "trumpet of God" (1 Corinthians 15:52; 1 Thessalonians 4:16-17). But if this were the same trumpet Jesus mentions in Matthew 24:31, the rapture of the church would, of necessity, have to occur at the *end* of the tribulation (post-trib), not prior to it (pre-trib).

Careful distinction must be made between these two trumpet blasts to avoid confusion about their specific timing. And as it relates to the rescue of Jesus' bride, timing is *everything*. The following comparisons/contrast are helpful here:

Rapture Trumpet

- Summons the elect of the church
- Calls the church into the air to meet Jesus
- Church goes immediately to heaven
- Occurs prior the tribulation, at the end of the church age
- Only the bride sees Christ
- Only the bride is mentioned

Second Coming Trumpet

- Gathers the elect of Israel
- Calls the Jews to Jerusalem to meet Jesus
- Jews travel to Jerusalem
- Occurs at the close of the tribulation

- All the world sees Christ

- Only Jewish people mentioned (no mention of the church)

THE PURPOSE OF GATHERING
THE JEWISH ELECT

Throughout the New Testament, we encounter the word "elect" (Greek *eklektos*) some 22 times. The word implies a prior choice by God of certain individuals for salvation. It's the same theological truth portrayed in the word *predestined* (Greek *proorizo*, meaning "to ordain beforehand"). While it is clear we must choose to believe in order to be saved, Scripture is equally clear that God's choice of his elect occurred "before the foundation of the world" (Ephesians 1:4), and before any of us had done anything "good or bad" (Romans 9:10-11). Without question, our salvation is according to his purpose, not our goodness or even our desire to be saved (John 1:12-13; Romans 9:11). In fact, for any of us to be saved, God *must* make the first move. Left to ourselves, we would never choose him because of our spiritual deadness and love for sin (John 6:44-45; 15:16; Romans 3:10-12; 8:29-30; Ephesians 2:1-4).

God's sovereign, unconditional choice of us (election) is arguably the most humbling doctrine in all of Christianity. And though some may debate the specific nature and relationship between his choice of us and ours of him, upon arrival in heaven, no one will pat himself on the back for getting there.

Salvation, as we will one day fully realize, is indeed *of the Lord* (Psalms 3:8; 37:39; Jonah 2:9). It belongs to him. It comes from him. And all praise for it goes back to him (Romans 11:36).

And here in Matthew 24:31, Jesus applies that salvation to the Jewish remnant who are alive at the end of the tribulation and the time of his return. The prophet Daniel describes it this way:

Now at that time Michael, the great prince who stands guard over the sons of your people, will arise. And there will be a time of distress such as never occurred since there was a nation until that time; and at that time your people, *everyone who is found written in the book, will be rescued* (Daniel 12:1).

Dr. Thomas Ice writes, "Christ, who apparently has this passage from the book of Daniel in mind, shortens the phrase 'everyone who is found written in the book' to 'the elect.'"[3] The book he refers to here is the "book of life" (Philippians 4:3; Revelation 3:5; 13:8; 17:8; 20:12, 15; 21:27).

These elect ones, according to the whole context of Matthew 24, appear to be Jews, as very Israel-centric language is used throughout (i.e., kingdom [verse 14], the holy place [verse 15], the Sabbath [verse 20], and the Messiah [verses 23-24]). [4]

TALKING 'BOUT MY GENERATION?

As Jesus maintains the same context and concept of the tribulation and his second coming, he next reveals what has become one of the most misunderstood and misinterpreted passages of Scripture in all of Bible prophecy:

Now learn the parable from the fig tree: when its branch has already become tender and puts forth its leaves, you know that summer is near; so, you too, when you see all these things, recognize that He is near, right at the door. Truly I say to you, *this generation* will not pass away until all these things take place. Heaven and earth will pass away, but My words will not pass away (Matthew 24:32-35).

Notice Jesus begins by calling his words a "parable." In fact, it would be one of five prophetic parables (or inspired illustrations or stories) related to the end times, the tribulation, and the subsequent times of rewards and judgments, as follows:

- The illustration of the fig tree (verses 32-35)
- The illustration of the days of Noah (verses 36-39)
- The illustration of the two men and two women (verses 40-41)
- The illustration of the faithful houseowner (verses 42-44)
- The illustration of the wise servant (verses 45-51)

Ever since the establishment of Israel as a nation on May 14, 1948, this passage has been widely interpreted to mean that within one generation after the fig tree (Israel) becomes a nation again (puts forth its leaves), Jesus will return at his second coming, and here's why: Some people interpret a biblical "generation" to be 40 years, based on the generation that wandered in the wilderness following the exodus from Egypt (Numbers 14:34). However, "generation" can also refer to a vast spectrum of time—from specific years to a generic, unspecified amount of time (Genesis 2:4; 5:1; 15:13, 16; Matthew 1:17; 12:39).

It is true that in Scripture, Israel is sometimes described symbolically as a fig tree (Judges 9:10-11; Jeremiah 8:13; Hosea 9:10; Habakkuk 3:17; Haggai 2:19; Matthew 21:19; Mark 11:13, 20-21; Luke 13:6-7). However, the question is whether Jesus is employing that symbolism here in Matthew 24:32-35. To find out, let's look more closely at this claim.

Obviously, Israel becoming a nation again is *the* game-changer of God's overall end-times narrative. It is the "super sign" of the last days. Concerning this, we all agree.

However, again, the critical question is whether that's the parallel

Jesus is making here. Those who hold to the belief that the fig tree in Matthew 24:32-35 is specifically Israel, that the putting forth of the leaves is Israel's rebirth, and that the generation is a specific length of time (40–80 years) tend to lean into general "date setting" for the coming of the Lord. But is that what Christ meant for his Olivet hearers (and us) to understand? I don't believe so.

To begin with, there is no direct correlation between the fig tree in Matthew 24:32-35 and Israel as a nation. In fact, Luke records a more complete version of Jesus' words: "He told them a parable: Behold the fig tree *and all the trees*; as soon as they put forth leaves..." (Luke 21:29).

To apply the same principle of interpretation here (i.e., a tree signifies a specific nation) would mean that "all the trees" must refer to "all the nations." But for all the nations to "put forth leaves" has no prophetic meaning or significance. So the fig tree = Israel interpretation doesn't hold up here.

Instead, the point Jesus is making is not about Israel as a nation, but rather, the fact that when a tree produces leaves, this signifies that "summer is near" (Matthew 24:32). Jesus uses an example of something his listeners know about (trees, seasons, fruit bearing) to explain something they *don't* know about (i.e., the significance of the tribulation events and how that applies to their lives and the time limits of the end-times narrative). He uses a principle from the world of nature to illustrate a truth about the nearness of his second coming during the tribulation.

Second, the "generation" in Jesus' story is the generation alive *at that time* (the time of the tribulation). Notice the characteristics of "this generation":

1. They will "see all these things" (Matthew 24:33). What things? The things he has just prophesied about in verses 4-31, or the happenings of the tribulation—false christs,

wars, famine, and the abomination of desolation. The world has seen none of these tribulation events to date.

2. That particular generation (the one that witnesses the abomination of desolation) can have the confidence that the return of Jesus to earth is "near, right at the door" (verse 33). Those believers alive at that time will see the *actual signs* of the last days be fulfilled before their eyes (the "birth pangs" of verse 8).

3. This generation (the tribulation generation) "will not pass away until all these things take place" (verse 34). In other words, the tribulation will not go on indefinitely. It will end in a timely manner, and this generation will be alive to see it. The tribulation will last only seven years, to be exact (cf. verse 22).

Put another way, the generation that witnesses the signs described in Matthew 24:4-31 will also witness the return of the Lord. Underneath this passage in my personal Bible, I have this note: "The generation that sees the *beginning* of the end will also witness the *end* of the end."

Therefore, the fig tree illustration is just that—an illustration, albeit a very powerful and prophetic one for those believers who are alive on earth during those days. It's a message of hope for them.

Jesus concludes by assuring his inner circle of disciples of the reliability of what he has just said: "Heaven and earth will pass away, but My words will not pass away" (verse 35).

Christ has just told them that the generation that witnesses the events of the tribulation will "*not pass away* until all these things take place." "This generation" = the tribulation generation, not a generation of years since Israel's birth in 1948.

Now Jesus uses the same phrase to describe two things that *will* pass away and one that will *not*. "Heaven and earth" (verse 35) essentially refers to all that God has made in the material universe—stars, planets, galaxies, and more. And we know from Peter's epistle that "the day of the Lord will come like a thief, in which the heavens will pass away [same Greek word] with a roar and the elements will be destroyed with intense heat, and the earth and its works will be burned up" (2 Peter 3:10). God will one day break apart the universe at the subatomic level, causing everything that is seen to dissolve into nothingness through an intense, heaven-fueled heat.

If there is anything ancient cultures considered to be consistent and unwavering, it's the heavens and the earth. The stability of our planet, our solar system and the surrounding galaxy is a foundation upon which all life depends. However, even these will not last forever. On the other hand, says Jesus of Nazareth, "My words will not pass away" (Matthew 24:35). Christ here makes the bold assertion that his words, including those found here in Matthew 24, will endure for all eternity. They are eternal because *he* is eternal.

Who could make such a statement but God alone? The surety of God's Word is *the* bedrock of the Christian faith. Some high-profile progressive pastors today have asserted that "because the Bible says so" is not convincing enough evidence to demonstrate the validity of Christianity and the resurrection. They claim our faith must not rest on "letters from 2,000 years ago."

But what these modern-day judges and Bible critics fail to understand (or simply refuse to acknowledge) is that without the divinely written revelation of Scripture, our faith lives in our hearts only as a subjective reality, not an objective, verifiable one. Jesus' words can be temporally denied or dismissed, but they can never be destroyed.

What *will* pass away are the futile speculations of darkened minds and the philosophical postulations of progressive preachers and theologians. What will *never* perish are the *words* of Jesus Christ. And where do we find these words faithfully and accurately documented?

You guessed it: *the Bible.*

Jesus himself declared, "I am the…truth" (John 14:6). Therefore, whatever comes from his mouth is 100 percent divine, trustworthy truth.

This is why he next warns against "date setting" in connection with his return: "That day and hour no one knows, not even the angels of heaven, nor the Son, but the Father alone" (Matthew 24:36).

Why would Jesus make a statement like this if, just a few sentences earlier, he had given us some supposed "secret clue" (fig tree = Israel's rebirth) as to when he would return? Obviously, he didn't.

Contextually, Jesus is referring here to his second coming, not the rapture. While the rapture is a signless event and its timing cannot be known or predicted, the physical return of Christ—spoken of in verses 29-31—*is* more seasonably predictable. Even so, the exact day and hour still won't be known. And this isn't the only place or time Jesus spoke of the unknown timing of his return. In fact, he repeated it two more times in the Olivet Discourse, and then again at his ascension event (Matthew 24:42; 25:13; Act 1:7). So it must be important to him that we not attempt to pinpoint the exact timing of his return.

And his words are still true today. No matter what supposed signs or hidden numbers, Jewish feasts, planetary alignments, visons, or dreams some people may propose, *no one* knows the day and the hour of his return, whether it refers the rapture or the second coming.

In fact, so secretive is this information that Jesus himself, during the time of his earthly ministry, didn't have access to that knowledge. As the unique God-man, he voluntarily chose to lay aside some of his heavenly privileges and prerogatives in order to (1) fully identify with humanity (Philippians 2:6-8; Hebrews 2:9; 2:17; 4:15) and (2) be fully dependent on the Father (John 7:16; 8:26, 28; 12:49; 14:10, 24; 31; 15:15). Of course, now that Christ is glorified in heaven at the right hand of the Father, he is fully restored to his previous glory and knows all things (Matthew 28:18; Hebrews 12:2).

THE UNPREDICTABLE MESSIAH

How arrogant are those today who essentially claim to know more than Jesus and to have somehow deciphered, decoded, or otherwise figured out the day of Christ's signless rapture when he explicitly stated that no one can know the hour of his second coming, which is preceded by multiple, specific precursors and signs.

Even with all the tribulation harbingers and signposts that point to Christ's return as described in Revelation, he will nonetheless come "like a thief" (1 Thessalonians 5:2; Revelation 16:15) and at "an hour when you do not think he will" (Matthew 24:43-44).

And when Christ does come back, humanity will witness a shocking display of divine wrath never before seen...with the possible exception of one past cataclysmic event, which we will explore in the next chapter.

CHAPTER 13

THE DAYS OF NOAH
ARE REVISITED

Matthew 24:37-41

The story of Noah and the global flood would have been familiar to the inner circle of disciples listening to Jesus as he taught the Olivet Discourse. It was an event of apocalyptic proportions, one not soon forgotten. In fact, in the ancient world, some 300 versions of the flood story were passed down through a multitude of cultures. However, the Jews were the only ones who recorded and recounted all its details, and accurately, as Moses was divinely inspired by God when he wrote the flood account in Genesis 6–8.

In modern times, the impact of the account of the global flood has subsided at the hands of critics and skeptics who deny its reality altogether. However, truth-seeking researchers and scientists are now having to revisit their previous ridicule of the story of Noah's ark due to recent discoveries and phenomenon. When Mount Saint Helens erupted in May 1980, the resulting catastrophic ripple effects produced a multitude of compressed rock and soil strata in just a matter of weeks that mirror similar striations found in other places, like the Grand Canyon, which scientists and archaeologists have long argued took "millions of ages" to form.[1]

In addition, a primary argument against a global flood has been that there could not possibly have been enough water to cover the entire earth in Noah's day (this, despite the fact our planet is 75 percent covered with water!). It is now believed that there are vast reservoirs of water beneath the earth's surface that hold four times the amount of water we presently see on Earth![2]

Others claim they have indeed found Noah's ark, or the fossilized, petrified remains of it.[3] Laying out in the open in the valley of Ararat, this "boat-shaped" object, or the outline of it, has sparked legendary tales in the region.

These ark hunters have also claimed to have discovered massive, stone boat anchors used by Noah, along with a supposed structure that seems to match the dimensions of the ark. While curious, I and others have yet to be convinced the evidence provided so far is conclusive. In our view, not enough credible, verifiable evidence has been presented that proves beyond a reasonable doubt that *the* ark has been found. Such a monumental archaeological discovery must, of necessity, be validated and verified, like other biblically relevant finds.

Though there are some similarities between the aforementioned half-buried object and the biblical ark (it nearly matches the dimensions of the ark, and it does reside in the mountains of Ararat), the evidence has yet to meet the criteria of irrefutable apologetic proof. It would seem that to be able to say that the actual ark has been found, the proof would need to be (1) accepted by Christian archaeologists and theologians alike, and (2) be blatantly obvious to an unbelieving and skeptical world.

This side of heaven, we may never conclusively know the exact location of the ark and know what remains of it, if anything. But should a convincing discovery ever be verified, it would be a mighty last-days apologetic, warning the world of another prophesied global judgment, which we read about in Revelation 6–19.

That said, Bible-believing Christians already embrace the historical reality of Noah, his ark, and the earth-covering flood—primarily because Moses, Jesus, the Gospel writers, and the apostles believed it. For if Jesus was wrong about Noah, then he could also be wrong about the end of the world, himself, and about your salvation and eternal destiny.

BACK TO THE FUTURE

So, what exactly does Jesus say about the days of Noah, and how does this serve as a prophetic precursor to his second coming? In Matthew 24:37-39, he says,

> The coming of the Son of Man will be just like the days of Noah. For as in those days before the flood they were eating and drinking, marrying and giving in marriage, until the day that Noah entered the ark, and they did not understand until the flood came and took them all away; so will the coming of the Son of Man be.

Several observations and further study are needed here for us to better grasp what the Lord is saying.

First, Jesus describes the everyday activities of the conceivably billions of people who lived in Noah's generation. The phrase "they were eating and drinking" perhaps alludes to people enjoying everyday life without a thought related to Noah's prophecies and preaching.

And the statement "they were marrying and giving in marriage" has been interpreted in varying ways with regard to what Jesus meant by these words.

View 1

View 1 is that the phrase simply means that people were going about their lives as usual. Just as they ate and drank each day, so they kept on getting married and being given (by the fathers) in marital unions. Nothing to see here. They were just occupied with life, uncaring and perhaps even uninformed about the coming flood. They were certainly unprepared for it, for, as we know, not one of them repented.

View 2

In view 2, some see a connection between Jesus' words and Genesis 6:1-3, which says, "Now it came about, when men began to multiply on the face of the land, and daughters were born to them, that the sons of God saw that the daughters of men were beautiful; and they took wives for themselves, whomever they chose. Then the LORD said, "My Spirit shall not strive with man forever, because he also is flesh; nevertheless his days shall be one hundred and twenty years.'"

Apparently, demonic entities or "sons of God" (Hebrew *bene elohim*) took for themselves mortal women as wives in what amounted to an unimaginable, perverse sexual union. One may ask how fallen angels, who are by nature spirit beings, could accomplish such a terrible task. But when we reach Genesis 18–19, we read about two angelic men, along with someone who seems to be a theophany (*theo* = God, *phanos* = to show) or a physical manifestation of God in human form. Whenever a theophany occurs in Scripture, he is typically referred to as "the angel of the LORD" (Genesis 16:7-12; 21:17-18; 22:11-18; Exodus 3:2; Judges 2:1-4; 5:23; 6:11-14; 13:3-22; 2 Samuel 24:16; Zechariah 1:12; 3:1; 12:8). Because this appears to be a role only the second member of the Godhead—the Son—fulfills, it is often referred to as a Christophany.

In the Genesis account, the two angels continue on toward Sodom to rescue Lot and his family before God pours out his fire-and-brimstone judgment on the cities in that region, which also included Gomorrah, Admah, and Zeboiim (Genesis 10:19; 14:2-3; Deuteronomy 29:23). However, when the angels show up at Lot's house, they appear as men with all the accompanying physical characteristics and abilities:

1. They are seen and perceived to be men (Genesis 19:1).

2. They had feet like men (verse 2).

3. They ate food like men (verse 3).

4. They could sleep (implied from verse 4).

5. They were believed to possess male genitalia (verse 5). The sodomites of Sodom, who included young and old (possibly evidence that pedophiles, or minor-attracted persons, were plentiful there), demanded that Lot bring out his male guests so that "we may have relations with them" (verse 5). The single Hebrew word translated "have relations" is *yada*, which, according to context, can mean anything from literal knowledge to having sexual intercourse. The word is used the latter way by Moses to describe Adam's sexual relations with wife Eve (Genesis 4:1, 25), Cain's relations with his wife (verse 17), and Lot's daughters, being virgins, who had "not had relations with man" (Genesis 19:8).

6. They could use physical force (verse 10).

7. They could speak like men (verses 12-13).

So we know from this account that angels possess the ability, at times, to take on human form. It is not known what happens to their bodies after they return to the spirit world.

This does not conclusively prove that this is what occurred in Genesis 6:1-3, with demons assuming physical form, but it is a real possibility. The phrase "took wives for themselves, whenever they chose" could imply some authority or force. Many Bible scholars believe, as I do, that because of this heinous sin committed during the days of Noah, God sentenced those sexually deviant demons to a special prison. This is likely who Jude was writing about in Jude 6-7, because the angels are contextually connected with Sodom and Gomorrah:

> Angels who did not keep their own domain, but abandoned their proper abode, He has kept in eternal bonds under darkness for the judgment of the great day, just as Sodom and Gomorrah and the cities around them, since they in the same way as these indulged in gross immorality and went after strange flesh, are exhibited as an example in undergoing the punishment of eternal fire (Jude 6-7; cf. Matthew 24:38).

The second view, then, sees Jesus as referring to demonic marriages, and carries much more of an evil overtone than the ordinary marriage practice of view one.

View 3

The third view stems from a rabbinical teaching about Genesis 6 that has its roots in the intertestamental period in Genesis 6. Some Jewish scholars who have studied about the days of Noah believe that homosexual marriages were performed during those days, and that wedding songs were composed for such ceremonies.[4]

Based on this understanding, these scholars conclude that this depth of depravity and abomination with regard to the sanctity of marriage was essentially the last straw for God, who then determined to send the flood. They also observe that, in the eyes of God, any civilization that practiced and celebrated marriage between people of the same sex lost its right to exist.[5]

Those are among the ways that the phrase "marrying and giving in marriage" (Matthew 24:38) is understood. And this activity continued up until the very day that Noah entered the ark. This indicates that during the time Noah built the ark, no one contemplated the severity of the prophesied coming judgment. They did not stop to consider how wicked and depraved it was to have sex with powerful demons. Nor did they repent from homosexual marital unions.

Today, "gay marriage" (which isn't marriage at all, but simply a new label applied to the ancient sin of sodomy) is legally practiced, celebrated, and defended in the United States, compliments of then-President Barack Obama and the Supreme Court of our land. In the court's 5–4 decision regarding *Obergefell v. Hodges*, the justices voted to redefine the concept of marriage itself by declaring homosexual relationships legitimate. With this decision, they justified the very sin for which God incinerated cities 3,000 years ago.

Concerning this historical heinous decision, Justice Samuel Alito wrote, "As far as I'm aware, until the end of the twentieth century, there was never a nation or a culture that recognized marriage between two people of the same sex."[6]

He was right.

If those Jewish scholars were right as well, then the last time a civilization celebrated gay marriage, God literally and permanently wiped them off the planet in divine, wrathful judgment.

What similar judgment awaits our country? And the world?

WHAT'S IN A NAME?

Jesus further draws upon the day of Noah with yet another attribute concerning that generation: "They did not understand until the flood came and took them all away; so will the coming of the Son of Man be" (Matthew 24:39).

Here, Christ makes it clear he fully believed in the flood account, its source (God), and its severity. And his point is that Noah's generation refused to believe judgment was imminent until it actually happened to them. To those wicked pagans, Noah was nothing more than a religious conspiracy theorist.

The word Jesus uses for "understand" primarily means "to know, recognize, or perceive." In other words, the people were clueless until "all the fountains of the great deep burst open, and the floodgates of the sky were opened" (Genesis 7:11). And just to lend more historical credibility to the account, Moses, in that same verse, even tells us the exact year, month, and day the flood began.

For at least two generations (or maybe more), Noah had been constructing his massive boat. And he wasn't the only preacher of righteousness in his day. His great-grandfather, Enoch, was also a righteous proclaimer who warned of coming judgment (Jude 14-15). And Enoch's son was Methuselah, whom we all know lived longer than any other human (969 years—Genesis 5:27).

However, you may not be aware of the prophetic meaning Enoch embedded within his son's name. *Methuselah* means "when he is gone, it shall come," or "his death shall bring it." But bring what? Let's crunch the numbers and find out.

We know from Genesis 7:6, 11 that the flood came in the six-hundredth year of Noah's life. And what is the significance of that? Not much, unless you also realize this was the exact same year that Methuselah died. When we do the simple math of the genealogies and years provided for us in Genesis 5:21-32 and 6:6, 11, we can calculate the year of Methuselah's death to be the same year "it came" (i.e., the flood).

Surely the meaning of Methuselah's name was not hidden from Noah's generation. But like Enoch, Lamech, and Noah, Methuselah was not just a godly man, but also very likely a vocal herald of righteousness, sin, God's provision, and the coming deluge. In fact, the Lord allowed this man with the prophetic name to live longer than any other human—almost a millennium! Why? So that with every mention of his name, the prophecy about future judgment would be repeated. Today, it would be like naming someone Armageddon, Rapture, or Revelation!

The name Methuselah in itself is evidence of God's patience and grace—as in 969 years of patience! And yet even with all those ancient clues and calls to repentance, every person of that time turned a blind eye and a deaf ear to those who warned of judgment.

As Jesus said, "They did not understand" (Matthew 24:39). They didn't take seriously the preachers, prophets, prophecies, and proclamations of their day. They were too busy, too preoccupied with self, selfish pursuits, and sin. They filled their minds, hearts, and schedules with so much worldly wickedness that not until the rain came pouring down on their heads and they heard the liquid explosions bursting out of the ground did they finally clue in. But it was too late. The hour and offer of salvation had expired. As for those who will one day gather at Armageddon and surround Jerusalem, the sudden appearance of the Son of Man will jolt them awake to the reality of their predicament. But again, it will be too late.

For Noah's generation, when the rain began to fall, the people discovered the door to the ark was closed and sealed. In fact, Noah and his family had already been inside the ark for seven days prior to the start of the flood (Genesis 7:7, 10).

But the people had ignored even that final warning. I have often pondered whether anyone noticed that the sounds coming from the ark's construction site had been strangely absent for seven days. Whether they wondered *Has anyone seen that Noah fellow lately?* Or, *Why are we suddenly seeing thousands of animals around here?*

Maybe not. We'll never know. But what we do know is that Noah, like someone running for cover at the sight of a tornado, had fled to safety, taking refuge with his family within the ark. The rest of humanity remained outside, oblivious as to what was about to hit them.

It was now official. The door of opportunity for salvation was now shut. The chance to repent had come to an end, and in this case, God himself had shut that door (Genesis 7:16).

"I WISH WE'D ALL BEEN READY"

This willful denial and rejection of prophetic truth reminds me of those who, in our day, mock, ridicule, and dismiss teachings about the rapture, tribulation, Antichrist, God's judgments, and the second coming of Jesus Christ. Peter warned us to expect these last-days deniers:

> Know this first of all, that in the last days mockers will come with their mocking, following after their own lusts, and saying, "Where is the promise of His coming? For ever since the fathers fell asleep, all continues just as it was from the beginning of creation." For when they maintain this, it escapes their notice that by the word of God the heavens existed long ago and the earth was formed out of water and by water, through which the world at that time was destroyed, being flooded with water. But by His word the present heavens and earth are being reserved for fire, kept for the day of judgment and destruction of ungodly men (2 Peter 3:3-7).

Peter's prophetic warning rings as true today as it did 2,000 years ago when the Holy Spirit inspired him to write it.

It is at this point that Jesus pivots, applying what happened in Noah's day to what will happen at the end of the world: "There will be two men in the field; one will be taken and one will be left. Two women will be grinding at the mill; one will be taken and one will be left" (Matthew 24:40-41).

This passage has been popularly interpreted as referring to the rapture of the church, primarily because the words Jesus used seem to fit with some being "taken" (up in the rapture), while the rest are "left" (behind on the earth). But is that what Jesus is saying here? I don't believe so, for the following reasons:

1. The Chronological Context

As we have seen, Jesus' Olivet Discourse is focused on the seven-year tribulation period. In fact, he has yet to say anything about the rapture at all. Why? Simply because his future audience are those Jews who will find themselves amid the "birth pangs" (Matthew 24:8) of wars (verses 6-7), false Christs (verses 4-5, 11), famine, earthquakes (verses 6-7), martyrdom (verse 9), persecution (verses 9-10), global lawlessness (verse 12), the gospel preached to the entire planet (verse 14), the abomination of desolation (verses 15-20), the "great tribulation" (verses 21-23), reported sightings of the Messiah's return (verses 24-26), and the actual return of Jesus (verses 27-31).

The setting, background, and events here all take place during the *tribulation*, during a post-rapture era that primarily involves Jewish-related themes. In fact, it is not until the following evening, on Thursday night, that Christ introduces the rapture and the future indwelling and ministry of the Holy Spirit—two mysterious, foreign concepts to those disciples living under the old covenant (John 14:1-3, 12, 16, 18; 16:7-15). These two promises were exclusively for the *church* (yet another mystery to them) and would be fulfilled exclusively during the church age. The indwelling of the Spirit began at Pentecost (Acts 2) and the rapture will occur at some future time, marking the end of the church age (1 Thessalonians 4:13-18). So the chronological context puts the passage in the tribulation, not at the time of the rapture.

2. The Immediate Context

Jesus had just finished describing what the Revelation generation will be like, using the days of Noah as his illustration. Then, in the *very next verse*, he says that some will be "taken," while others will be "left." Who is who here? Who are the ones taken? Are they taken up in the rapture? No, they are taken *away* in judgment. Look at Matthew 24:39. The ones taken in Noah's day were taken away in *judgment* through the flood. Now look at verses 40-41. One man in the field will be "taken." One woman grinding at the mill will be "taken."

The single Greek word in Matthew 24:39 translated "took them all away" (*airo*) can mean to "raise, take up, or lift" and is used in the New Testament to refer to picking up something or someone (Matthew 4:6; 9:6; 14:20; 16:24; 21:21; Mark 2:3; 4:15; 6:29). The word can also mean to "take away," which is the nuance here. However, interpreting the passage based on original word meaning alone would place the rapture at the close of the tribulation.

Further, the problem is that no one would argue that those in Noah's day were "raptured" upward and saved from the flood. On the contrary, the word here clearly means to be taken *away in judgment*.

Jesus taught that same meaning to his disciples:

> I tell you, on that night there will be two in one bed; one will be taken and the other will be left. There will be two women grinding at the same place; one will be taken and the other will be left. [Two men will be in the field; one will be taken and the other will be left] (Luke 17:34-36).

Notice the disciples' follow-up question: "Where, Lord?" (verse 37). That is, where will they be taken? Jesus' answer is specific: "Where the body is, there also the vultures will be gathered" (verse 37).

That doesn't sound to me like being raptured to heaven!

Christ is undoubtedly referring to Armageddon and the brutal slaughter he will bring at that time. It is there that all the vultures and birds of the air will "assemble for the great supper of God, so that you may eat the flesh of kings and the flesh of commanders and the flesh of mighty men and the flesh of horses and of those who sit on them and the flesh of all men, both free men and slaves, and small and great" (Revelation 19:17-18; cf. Matthew 24:28).

So, the immediate context (i.e., the flood judgment) is that those "taken" are taken to judgment at the second coming, and those "left" behind are the righteous ones who remain alive and will be received into Christ's millennial kingdom (Matthew 25:34).

As mentioned, interpreting this as a rapture passage places the timing of that event at the end of the tribulation, not prior to it.

This is what's known as the post-tribulational rapture view. However, this belief doesn't square with the Scripture passages that promise the church will be delivered *before* the coming tribulation wrath (1 Thessalonians 1:10; 5:9; Revelation 3:10).

Also, during the time of God's wrath in Revelation, we never see the bride of Christ anywhere except heaven. The word *ecclesia* ("church") occurs nowhere in Revelation 6–19, the very time of God's outpouring of fury and anger upon those who dwell on the earth. On the contrary, we see the church in heaven, worshipping the Lord, being rewarded, celebrating the marriage of the Lamb, and returning *with* Christ *from* heaven at the end of the tribulation (Revelation 4:4, 10-11; 19:7-9, 14). Additionally, if the post-tribulational rapture were true, how do you account for the righteous Gentiles Jesus invites into his kingdom following his second coming and the sheep and goats judgment in Matthew 25:31-40? If the rapture occurred at the close of the tribulation, these saints would already have their glorified bodies, as they would surely have been raptured with the rest of the saints. And yet Jesus' words indicate no rapture for them, but that they come into the kingdom in their mortal bodies.

So are we now living in days like the days of Noah? Well, yes and no. No in the absolute sense of Jesus' words in the Olivet Discourse. His prophecy will not be ultimately fulfilled until the tribulation and second coming.

But yes in the sense that our generation is rapidly resembling the one alive in Noah's day.

With the continued descent into depravity, godlessness, sexual deviancy, violence, and an obsessive preoccupation with self and everyday pursuits, I believe we, too, are bringing sorrow and grief to God's heart, just as Noah's generation did (see Genesis 6:6).

But as Genesis 6 also states, after God's sorrow comes his judgment.

PART 4

HOW SHOULD LAST DAYS' BELIEVERS PREPARE?

CHAPTER 14

BE ON THE ALERT

Matthew 24:42-44

Many years ago, when bumper stickers were still in vogue, hardly a car on the road was without at least one or two mini-billboards decorating the rear panels or bumper. These signs stared you in the face as you followed the car in front of you. And they touched on a wide variety of subjects, including politics, humor, pop culture, music, sports, and religion.

Among them also were those that silently broadcasted messages about Jesus, including some about his return to planet Earth. One popular bumper sticker read,

JESUS IS COMING SOON
ARE YOU READY?

That was a loose but fairly accurate paraphrase of Christ's words in Matthew 24:42-44, which he began with this warning: "Therefore be on the alert, for you do not know which day your Lord is coming."

CAFFEINE FOR THE SOUL

There is much we can learn from Jesus' message here, so let's begin where he does—with the word "therefore." Here, the Lord is making a concluding statement. He has just told his disciples about world conditions at the time of the second coming, and how they will parallel the days of Noah (Matthew 24:36-39). At the close of that "was/will be" comparison, he specifies how everyone at that time will be separated into two categories: (1) the taken, and (2) the left behind. As we saw in the previous chapter, those who are taken will be swept away into God's judgment, while those who are left here on Earth will continue on into Jesus' millennial kingdom.

"With this in mind," Christ says, "be ready, because the exact timing of my return cannot be known."

Let's unpack this verse so we can have a more complete understanding of it.

First, Jesus is speaking here only to believers ("*your* Lord"). His concern at this time is not for those who remain in a state of defiant unbelief after seven years of judgments and wrath. By this point, late in the tribulation, Scripture indicates that a person's destiny has already been determined (Revelation 14:9-11). We know that during the early part of the tribulation, following the rapture, there will be a massive spiritual revival in which people turn to faith in Christ (Revelation 7:9). An unknown but significant percentage of these will pay for their faith with their lives (Revelation 6:9-11). Revelation 20:4 also reveals that, following the implementation of the beast's mark (666), many more will lose their lives, martyred for Jesus through beheading.

We can also discern from Scripture that, due to the enforcement of that same mark of the beast, Antichrist will also make his own separation of humanity into two groups: (1) the marked and (2) the unmarked. With this global economic *and* religious mandate, earth's population will be divided into these two categories—saved (unmarked) or unsaved (marked). And just as all who are saved are guaranteed eternal life in heaven (Ephesians 1:13-14), so all those who receive the mark are similarly sealed and irreversibly marked for damnation and eternal torment in the lake of fire (Revelation 14:9-11).

So the exhortation to "be on the alert" in Matthew 24:42 applies only to believers in Yeshua (primarily, if not exclusively Jews) who are alive on earth during the final months of the seven-year tribulation period.

Second, let's look at the meaning of the command itself. The phrase "be on the alert" is one word in the New Testament Greek text, *gregoreuo*, and it literally means to "stay awake." It's the same word Jesus would use just one day later, when, in the Garden of Gethsemane, he told his disciples to "remain here and *keep watch* with Me" (Matthew 26:38; cf. verses 40-41). Paul also uses the word to encourage the Thessalonian believers, who struggled to keep faith in the midst of persecution and false teaching regarding the rapture. Paul instructed them to "not sleep as others do, but let us be *alert* and sober" (1 Thessalonians 5:6). And it's the word Jesus himself would later use to jolt the church at Sardis back into a vibrant relationship with him: "*Wake up*, and strengthen the things that remain…if you do not wake up, I will come like a thief, and you will not know at what hour I will come upon you" (Revelation 3:2-3).

The last time the word is used is in Revelation 16:15, where the Lord declares, "Behold, I am coming like a thief. Blessed is the one who *stays awake* and keeps his clothes, so that he will not walk about naked and men will not see his shame."

While the literal meaning of "be on the alert" is to be physically awake, the broader and more directly applicable meaning is to be vigilant and watchful. As the terrible judgments of the tribulation's second half become more intense, and Antichrist's kingdom begins to crumble (Revelation 17–18), the temptation may be for these believers to lose heart and not persevere to the end (Matthew 24:13). But Jesus says just the opposite should occur: "When these things [the final signs of the tribulation] begin to take place, straighten up and lift your heads, because your redemption is drawing near" (Luke 21:28).

For those tribulation believers, hope is an anchor, keeping them tethered to their soon deliverance by Messiah.

The third observation we can make from Matthew 24:42 is that the precise day of their Lord's return cannot be known. Jesus did not know nor announce the exact day of his second-coming arrival. He had already said this earlier in verse 36, but now he repeats it here for emphasis. Why? I believe we can discern a threefold explanation for this revelation.

First, Jesus had already told the disciples of detailed supernatural signs that would occur at the beginning (Matthew 24:3-14), midpoint (verses 15-26), and end of the tribulation (verses 27-31).

Together, false Christs as well as the Antichrist will attempt to lure the Jews out of hiding at this time in a final effort to annihilate them, which would prevent them from calling upon the Messiah to return and rescue them (Matthew 23:39; 24:4-5, 23-26; cf. Zechariah 12:10; Romans 11:26). Not knowing the day of his return and yet watching for the signs will help keep them alert until his actual coming.

Second, had Jesus given a precise date on some future prophetic calendar, it would have negated the necessity of his followers being on the alert. Knowing the day of his coming would only tempt those end-times disciples into lethargy and spiritual slumber. This accusation is often made against those (such as myself) who hold belief in a pre-trib rapture. Critics of the pre-trib view claim that believing in the imminent rescue of the bride only leads to laziness. But in fact, the exact opposite is true. Believing that Jesus could come back at any time (called the doctrine of *imminency*) causes us to be alert and watchful, not lethargic and uncaring. At the same time, I would argue that those who claim to know the precise timing of the rapture at either the midpoint or end of the tribulation are much more likely to fall into spiritual slumber until immediately prior to his coming.

But regardless of one's view of the rapture's timing, we all still need to be reminded to stay awake and be alert, whether it be in this age (for the rapture) or during the coming tribulation era (for the second coming).

Third, the second coming, *unlike* the rapture, is an event preceded by a multitude of signs, many of which we have already studied in Matthew 24. Revelation 6–19 provides us a full "script of signs" preceding Christ's glorious return. There, we are foretold of 21 global billboards, better known as the seal, trumpet and bowl judgments. We learn of Antichrist, the false prophet, the abomination of desolation, the mark of the beast, and much more. And *all* these signs point to one person and one event—the second coming of Jesus Christ.

And yet, even with all these flashing road markers in Revelation, the precise day of Christ's return will still be unrevealed and unpredictable—until it actually happens. Were some Jewish or Gentile believers living during the tribulation to attempt to calculate (via prophecies and end-times signs) the exact day of Jesus' return, they would fail. Why? Because Jesus didn't stutter when he said, "Of that day and hour no one knows," and "You do not know which day your Lord is coming" (Matthew 24:36, 42).

That said, is it still possible for tribulation-era believers to know the *season* of his coming? Yes, I believe they will be able to. When the Lord sends the final round of judgments as described in Revelation 16 (the bowl judgments), that will be a pretty good indication that his return is rapidly approaching. And when much of the world goes completely dark with cosmic disturbances and the world's military forces are assembling in Israel, *that's* when Jesus says it's about to go down. That's also when these last-days Jewish believers can stand tall and lift their heads, because their redemption is drawing near... as in *any day now* (Luke 21:28).

Can you now see how arrogant, unbiblical, and utterly futile it is for anyone today to try to pinpoint the day of the rapture? If no one living during the tribulation will know—after dozens of supernatural apocalyptic signs—when the *second coming* will take place, how could we ever predict the rapture, which is preceded by *zero* signs? Even so, every year, self-proclaimed prophets attempt to "predict" the day of blessed hope based on Jewish feasts, planetary alignments, end-times prophecies, geopolitical occurences, global crises, a personal dream, supposed vision, or some other claimed divine revelation. But according to Scripture, the only thing we can be sure of is that their faux prophecies will fail, just like all similar previous predictions. All this does is to further inspire scoffers who subsequently emerge from the shadows, mocking not only the rapture but Christians and their Christ as well. This is yet another reason we desperately need to continue pursuing biblical discernment and immerse ourselves in the Scriptures. This way, we, like our Jewish brethren during the tribulation, will obey Jesus' command to "see to it that no one misleads you" (Matthew 24:4).

LIKE A THIEF

In Matthew 24:43-44, Jesus gives the briefest of parables to illustrate his point concerning (1) the level of alertness he desires his tribulation disciples to have, and (2) the fact the day of his arrival is unknown. This is among his shortest symbolic stories, yet one that contains profound truth and application.

In this, as well as in other prophetic parables, Jesus turns his attention to helping future tribulation believers make themselves ready for their Lord's return. We've already seen his admonition to "be on the alert" (verse 42), and now he illustrates his point with a story:

> Be sure of this, that if the head of the house had known at what time of the night the thief was coming, he would have been on the alert and would not have allowed his house to be broken into. For this reason you also must be ready; for the Son of Man is coming at an hour when you do not think He will (Matthew 24:43-44).

Here, Jesus teaches with clarity and simplicity. The point of the parable is obvious. If a thief were to announce his arrival ahead of time, the owner of the house "would not have allowed his house to be broken into."

Years ago, when our children were preteens, we went to see a movie one winter's evening. Upon our return home, we discovered that our house had been broken into, with thousands of dollars of personal possessions stolen. Had we known this would happen, we wouldn't have left, but rather, been fully prepared to "greet" the thief or thieves!

But that's the nature of thievery, isn't it? It happens at a time you don't expect. It's difficult to be on the alert for something you don't expect to happen. Today, so many professing Christians are functionally illiterate with regard to the Bible and possess little or no knowledge about Christ's return. It comes as no surprise, then, that there is very little of a "spirit of expectation" for the return of Jesus in the church. Very little eager anticipation to be snatched away at the rapture and taken by the Groom to the Father's house. Very little maranatha excitement as the early church exhibited.

In this passage, Jesus forecasts the *fact* of his second coming arrival ("your Lord *is coming*"), but not the exact *timing* of it. And because tribulation-era believers won't have that information, he wants them to always be on alert, and to "be ready" (verse 44), adding that "the Son of Man is coming at an hour when you do not think he will."

Dr. Thomas Ice notes, "Israel was not prepared and ready when Christ came the first time, but the remnant will be prepared and ready when he arrives the second time."[1]

We see clearly in Matthew 24:42, 44 that God places a high value on his children being alert and ready for his Son's return—whether it be for the bride waiting for the rapture, or the Jewish remnant watching for the second coming.[2]

EYES WIDE OPEN

About ten years ago, when I first began focusing my teaching and writing ministries on the doctrine of eschatology, I discovered the vast majority of Christians and churches to be in a state of ignorance, apathy, and unpreparedness. Like an old Western ghost town, their understanding of the end times was dilapidated and outdated. In fact, many had never heard of the Bible's inspiring teachings regarding the last days. Further, they were unaware of the fact that close to one-third of the Bible was prophetic at the time it was written. Others, including some pastors, simply didn't care, as there were many "more important and essential doctrines" to teach and study. Because of this, hardly any of them were "looking for the blessed hope," or "eagerly wait[ing] for a Savior" to return from heaven to gather them up to glory (Titus 2:13; Philippians 3:20).

However, by God's grace, and through a Holy Spirit-fueled movement of faithful pastors, teachers, and ministries, I am beginning to see a remnant awakening within the body of Christ. Believers worldwide are opening their eyes and hearts to the hopeful message inherent within Bible prophecy. Both old and young are discovering a newfound depth and a discernment in the Scriptures that they never knew existed. Because of this, their witness to the world is being renewed and broadened. And a passion for their coming Bridegroom has ignited.

May that flame not grow dim or be extinguished. Rather, may it grow and spread, catching fire in the hearts of Jesus' bride worldwide.

Alert—open eyes.

Attentive—discerning minds.

Ready—eager hearts.

Yes, Jesus *is* coming! Even so, come, Lord Jesus!

CHAPTER 15

BE A FAITHFUL
STEWARD

Matthew 24:45-51

J esus has now transitioned from a historical narrative in Matthew
24:36-39 to what is known as parabolic teaching in verses 40
and following. But these are not bedtime stories meant to entertain us. Rather, they are divine mandates meant to motivate us. As
the judgments of God greatly intensify during the latter half of the
tribulation, so Satan will also escalate his attacks on the Jewish remnant. Revelation 12 outlines for us the threefold strategy that he—
the "dragon"—will employ during the remaining 1,260 days of what
Jesus called the "*great* tribulation" (Matthew 24:21).

Whether in that future day or in ours, all opposition to our faith,
including direct persecution, tests the believer's mettle, revealing just
how resilient we are while facing ongoing adversity. As we've discovered, all those who embrace faith in Jesus during the tribulation will
suffer the wrath of man in a world gone mad with hatred toward
Christians and their God. And as we have also seen, there will be a
massive explosion of evangelism during the first half of the tribulation, with millions of Gentiles coming to faith in Christ. However,
those Gentile believers do not threaten Antichrist's reign in the same
way that the believing Jewish remnant does.

God's focus, especially during the final years and months of the tribulation, will be Israel, particularly the converted one-third of the Jews who remain in hiding (Zechariah 13:8). It is they who will be brought through the fire (verse 9) and respond to God's invitation: "Call on My name, and I will answer them; I will say, 'They are my people,' and they will say, 'The Lord is my God'" (verse 9; cf. Zechariah 12:10; Ezekiel 20:33-38; Matthew 23:38-39; Romans 11:26).

Because of the unprecedented challenges and persecution those Jewish believers will face, faithfulness to their Messiah will be critical and essential. Jesus therefore tells them this sobering parable:

> Who then is the faithful and sensible slave whom his master put in charge of his household to give them their food at the proper time? Blessed is that slave whom his master finds so doing when he comes. Truly I say to you that he will put him in charge of all his possessions. But if that evil slave says in his heart, "My master is not coming for a long time," and he begins to beat his fellow slaves, and eat and drink with drunkards; the master of that slave will come on a day that he does not expect him and at an hour which he does not know, and he will cut him in pieces and assign him a place with the hypocrites; in that place there will be weeping and gnashing of teeth (Matthew 24:45-51).

Certainly, the virtue of faithfulness is something for which all believers in all ages should strive. But here, we will see its primary application to the tribulation-era Jewish brethren, while also making personal application to our own lives as well.

A GOLDEN OPPORTUNITY

When Jesus entered Jerusalem on Palm Sunday, he officially presented himself to the nation of Israel as their King, and the people indicated they would receive him as such. Luke documents the crowd's response:

> As soon as He was approaching, near the descent of the Mount of Olives, the whole crowd of the disciples began to praise God joyfully with a loud voice for all the miracles which they had seen, shouting:
>
> "Blessed is the King who comes in the name of the Lord; peace in heaven and glory in the highest!" (Luke 19:37-38).

This was a good sign, for it indicated an openness and willingness to receive the Lord Jesus for who he was—the promised Messiah.

However, some of the Pharisees (Jewish religious leaders who exercised great dominance and influence over the people) objected, telling Jesus, "Teacher, rebuke your disciples" (verse 39).

The Lord responded, "I tell you, if these become silent, the stones will cry out!" (verse 40).

In essence, Jesus was saying, "Even the rocks of Israel [which weren't even alive] recognize who I am and would celebrate my arrival." You could argue that Christ was not-so-subtly warning the Pharisees, "Don't be *as dumb as a rock*. Recognize and receive your Messiah!"

What happened next is not only an often-overlooked scene, but also a dramatic and pivotal moment in Israel's history. As Jesus descended the Mount of Olives, he approached Jerusalem, and wept over the city, saying, "If you had known *this day*, even you, the things which make for peace! But now they have been hidden from your eyes" (verses 41-42).

Here, the heart of our Savior is laid bare, and we see the compassion and love he has for his people and his beloved Jerusalem. The same sentiment is also seen in Matthew 23:37, when he lamented over the city.

Following these words, Jesus again prophesied the coming destruction of Jerusalem and the temple:

The days will come upon you when your enemies will throw up a barricade against you, and surround you and hem you in on every side, and they will level you to the ground and your children within you, and they will not leave in you one stone upon another, because you did not recognize the time of your visitation (Luke 19:43-44).

As previously noted, if you visit the Western wall of the temple area today, you can still see some of the giant stones that the Roman army hurled down when they destroyed the temple structures.

And why did all this happen? Christ gave the answer: "Because you did not recognize the time of your visitation" (verse 44).[1]

FAILING THE TEST

In Jesus' parable in Matthew 24:45-51, we find these main elements:

The "master" is God.

The "household" is Israel.

The "faithful and sensible slave" represents the leadership of Israel.

Sadly, the Pharisees and scribes, with their personal and religious corruption, failed to "give them [the household of Israel] food at the proper time"—that is, to recognize the Messiah at his first coming (Matthew 16:1-4). Matthew recounts for us an earlier confrontation Jesus had with Israel's religious elites:

The Pharisees and Sadducees came up, and testing Jesus, they asked Him to show them a sign from heaven. But He replied to them, "When it is evening, you say, '*It will be* fair weather, for the sky is red.' And in the morning, '*There will be* a storm today, for the sky is red and threatening.' Do you know how to discern the appearance of the sky, but cannot *discern* the signs of the times? An evil and adulterous generation seeks after a sign; and a sign will not be given it, except the sign of Jonah." And He left them and went away.

One of the great lessons we learned from our Lord is that no matter how powerful, influential, or intimidating a person or institution may be, he always exhibited boldness and confidence before them because he was filled with discernment and truth. And nowhere was that demonstrated more clearly than in his repeated dealings with Israel's religious ruling class. Jesus essentially delivered a four-pronged rebuke to them. Translated, we could summarize the rebuke as follows:

1. They could discern lesser things, like the weather, but were failures at discerning the most important things, like the Messiah's arrival (Matthew 16:1-3).

2. They were an evil, unfaithful generation because they would rather seek signs instead of accepting the Savior. The fact that they had not already believed in him as a result of his earlier miracles indicated they had no intention of recognizing him as their Messiah and God. They wanted a supernatural miracle, and instead, Jesus pointed them to Scripture as his authenticating sign (Luke 16:31). They had already asked this same question earlier in Matthew 12:38-40, and Jesus gave them the same answer then as well.

3. They should have been experts on "the signs of the times." They studied the Scriptures and were considered experienced teachers in the Jewish law. Their job was to prepare the people for the first coming of the Lord and the presentation of him as their Messiah. However, they totally missed the signs of the times even when *the* sign of the times was physically and visibly standing a few feet in front of them!

4. Jesus turned and walked away, communicating, "This conversation is officially over." His refusal to continue engaging them in a pointless discussion was Jesus' way of not casting pearls before swine (Matthew 7:6). They were not worthy, nor were they ready, to receive the truth from him.

Later, Jesus would deliver his most scathing rebuke, in which he thoroughly discredited and dismantled them (Matthew 23:1-36).

These religious leaders were experts in legalism and hypocrisy, but amateurs in Bible prophecy. Like the evil slave in this parable, they religiously rationalized, "My master is not coming for a long time" (Matthew 24:48). Instead of leading Israel to faith in God and expectation of Messiah's coming, they laid a crushing burden of extra religious laws on the backs of the common Jew (verse 49). This is the very reason Jesus declared in Matthew 11:28-30, "Come to Me, all who are weary and heavy laden, and I will give you rest. Take My yoke upon you and learn from Me, for I am gentle and humble in heart, and you will find rest for your souls. For My yoke it easy and My burden is light."

So what awaits those future Jewish religious leaders? Christ's second coming will be unexpected for them, and the Master will assign them "a place with the hypocrites; in that place there will be weeping and gnashing of teeth" (Matthew 24:51).

Now we can better understand why this is such a sobering parable. But why is Jesus applying it to the tribulation-era Jewish disciples? So that they wouldn't repeat the mistakes of their first-century Jewish leaders and ancestors. Translated, "Don't miss me at my *second* coming the way they missed me at my *first*."

And the way to avoid that tragic error, Jesus counsels, is to be a "faithful and sensible" slave. Being faithful means to demonstrate loyalty and allegiance, especially during what we know will be incredibly difficult days for those Jewish believers. The word "sensible" (Greek *phronimous*) is used elsewhere by Christ to describe someone who is wise. This person, Christ says, "hears these words of Mine and acts upon them." He "may be compared to a wise man who built his house on the rock. And the rain fell, and the floods came, and the winds blew and slammed against that house, and yet it did not fall, for it had been founded on the rock" (Matthew 7:24-25).

We all face many challenges and storms in this life. Some threaten our physical possessions and well-being, including job losses, money problems, and illnesses and diseases. Or we may face struggles relating to our emotions and mental health—anxiety, depression, anger, confusion. Still other storms "burst" against us spiritually, disturbing and endangering our faith—doubt, sin, apathy, lack of biblical discernment.

To keep our "house" intact and standing, we must intentionally, actively, and consistently build it on the rock-solid words of Jesus of Nazareth. And if we need to be that kind of faithful and wise slave now, imagine how much more difficult circumstances will be for our Jewish brothers and sisters during earth's final days. They will face the psychological torture and spiritual warfare of Antichrist as they strive to maintain their loyalty to Messiah while patiently waiting for his return.

STRONG TO THE FINISH

For those future believers, it won't matter how much money is in their bank accounts, what kind of car they drive, where they live, or how many followers they have on social media. In terms of worldly achievements, their "success" will be irrelevant. In fact, the world will surely view them all as losers and nobodies.

But nowhere in Scripture does God call any of us to success. That's because the *results* of what we do for our Lord are entirely up to him. He is in charge of the outcome. What he *does* look for, and require, is *faithfulness* from his children.

No one knew this better than the apostle Paul, as documented in his first letter to the Corinthian church:

> Let a man regard us in this manner, as servants of Christ and stewards of the mysteries of God. In this case, moreover, it is required of stewards that one be found trustworthy. But to me it is a very small thing that I may be examined by you, or by any human court; in fact, I do not even examine myself. For I am conscious of nothing against myself, yet I am not by this acquitted; but the one who examines me is the Lord. Therefore do not go on passing judgment before the time, but wait until the Lord comes who will both bring to light the things hidden in the darkness and disclose the motives of men's hearts; and then each man's praise will come to him from God (1 Corinthians 4:1-5).

Paul is teaching that a person's opinion of you or me is "a very small [insignificant] thing." What matters most is God's opinion and evaluation. His approval is the prize we're looking for. And our faithfulness is nowhere more critical than when it comes to how we view and revere God's Word.

We are living in a culture drowning in lies. The truth is rarely respected or believed today. Virtually everything we read, hear, and see in movies, television shows, books, the internet, social media, the news, and from the government is tainted and poisoned with a cocktail of counterfeit truths and blatant lies. The only source of absolute truth and wisdom we can fully rely on is the Word of God. It is our guide, our template, and our GPS in a world gone insane and mired deep in deception and delusion. Faithfulness to what our Master says in his Word is what will see us through to the end. We need the Word now more than ever. And in the final days of the coming tribulation, Satan's greatest and most powerful lies will embed themselves deep within the minds and consciences of billions who worship his Antichrist. But the righteous Jewish remnant will recognize that the time of their visitation is close at hand. For this reason, they will saturate themselves in the Scriptures, and in doing so, they will prepare their hearts to meet their Messiah.

CHAPTER 16

BE AWAKE

Matthew 25:1-13

My good friend Olivier Melnick has a coffee mug that reads, "I can do all things through a verse taken out of context." How true! As Christians, in our eagerness to apply Scripture to our lives, we can sometimes inadvertently skip over the part where we discover what a verse or passage actually means. And without knowing what it means, our personal application can become misguided, mistaken, and sometimes even *made up*.

For example, suppose the people at your workplace are in a team meeting at work. Your boss speaks to the marketing department about submitting a concise monthly sales report, and says, "I would like to see you put things in a more *orderly* format." Suppose an employee who happens to serve in human resources hears the boss's words, then immediately leaves the room to go clean his office and desktop. After a few minutes, the boss walks into that person's office and says, "What are you doing?" To which the employee responds, "You just told us to put things in an orderly format, so that's what I'm doing."

"Well," the boss replies, "I do appreciate your eagerness. And being orderly is an important thing for everyone. However, first, I was referring to monthly sales reports, not individual offices. And second, I wasn't even speaking to you at all, but to marketing. I had something completely different to say to the human resources department. But you missed it because you left the room!"

Oops.

This same interpretive principle applies to the next parable Christ tells his disciples. In order to accurately understand any verse or passage of Scripture, we must first discover what it meant for the original hearers or readers. Only after finding that *one* primary meaning can we then make a correct application to our lives today. Failure to do this in Bible study undermines God's purpose for his Word and hijacks his intentions for our lives. It also twists Scripture, making it say things it was never intended to.

By way of reminder, Matthew 25 naturally flows from the end of Matthew 24. Jesus is simply continuing his Olivet Discourse regarding the end of days. Also, you may recall that when Matthew wrote his Gospel, there were no chapter divisions in Scripture. Rather, the chapter divisions were arranged and added around AD 1227 by a man named Stephen Langton, an archbishop of Canterbury. The Wycliffe Bible (1382) was the first to include these divisions.[1] So upon finishing Matthew 24:51, we pick up Jesus' next thought in Matthew 25:1.

A LESSON IN MISSING THE POINT

In the well-known parable of the ten virgins found in Matthew 25:1-13, Jesus tells the story of young maidens who take their lamps and go to meet the bridegroom. Five of the virgins are described as "prudent" and were prepared, evidenced by the fact that they had brought flasks of oil along with their lamps in the event the bridegroom's arrival was delayed. However, the other five, described as "foolish," took no extra oil with them. Then unexpectedly, at midnight, there was a shout, "Behold, the bridegroom! Come out to meet him" (verse 6).

Jesus goes on to explain that the unprepared bridesmaids attempted to borrow oil from the others because their lamps were burning out. However, their request is refused. Suddenly, the bridegroom arrives and takes the prepared virgins with him to the wedding feast, whereupon the door to the feast was shut.

Jesus then explains the application in verses 11 through 13:

> Later the other virgins also came, saying, "Lord, Lord, open up for us."
>
> But he answered, "Truly I say to you, I do not know you."
>
> Be on the alert then, for you do not know the day nor the hour.

Sadly, this parable is often cited as an illustration of the rapture of the church. And as we have seen, the rapture is not found in the context of the Olivet Discourse. This parable has also been used in an attempt to justify the partial-rapture theory, or the belief that only some Christians will be taken at the rapture, while other believers will be left behind. It is said that those Christians who are taken are those who are prepared and godly, while others are unprepared and perhaps even living in sin.

But there are several glaring inconsistencies with this view, as well as good reasons why this parable is not referring to the rapture.

First, nowhere in the New Testament do we see the concept of a partial rapture taught or even implied. On the contrary, 1 Corinthians 15:51 clearly states that at the rapture, "we will *all* be changed." As Christians, all our sins have been forgiven, and we are forever made righteous in the Lord's sight (2 Corinthians 5:21; Romans 5:1; 8:1; Hebrews 7:25). No scripture passage reverses or nullifies the perfect and holy standing we have before God. To think or teach that Jesus would punish his precious bride by forcing some believers to endure the awful tribulation wrath of God is both unthinkable and unbiblical.

Second, the church is pictured as the bride of Christ in the New Testament (Ephesians 5:25-26; Revelation 19:7). However, here in this parable, the subjects are the *attendants* of the bride (virgins), *not* the bride herself. In fact, the bride isn't even mentioned! So the comparison doesn't match and the parallel cannot be justified.

Third, in this parable, the Lord responds to the unprepared virgins in the same way he does to *un*believers in Matthew 7:21-23—he bars their entrance into heaven and the kingdom. Implicit in Jesus' words is that they are cast into hell (Matthew 24:50-51). This, too, would keep us from interpreting the parable as referring to a partial rapture. However, at the second coming of Christ, which leads to the *millennial kingdom* (and is the context of this parable—Matthew 25:1), there *will* be judgments that result in condemnation (Ezekiel 20:34-38; Matthew 24:40-51). Following the rapture, we will go immediately to the "Father's house," or heaven (John 14:1-3). But following the second coming, all believers will be ushered into the earthly millennial kingdom (Revelation 20:4-6). At both prophetic events, all believers without exception will go into the presence of God, whether in heaven (rapture) or on earth into the kingdom (return). And of course, previously raptured saints will accompany Jesus at his second coming, and then join the tribulation believers in the millennial kingdom (Revelation 19:8, 14).

Fourth, the entire context of Jesus' Olivet Discourse (Matthew 24–25) concerns his Jewish brethren during the time of the seven-year tribulation. Therefore, the *interpretation* of this parable must also be applied to those Jews living during that time. Jesus isn't referring here to pre-tribulation believers living in the church age (us). Like the boss in the illustration, he is specifically speaking to another group of believers. However, many Jews *will* believe in the Messiah during the tribulation and thus (in this parable) are urged to be prepared for Christ's second coming. Others will remain in unbelief, side with Antichrist, and be shut out of the kingdom.

Having said this, I strongly believe the New Testament teaches a pre-tribulation rapture of the church, meaning that Christ will return for his bride *prior* to the seven-year season of God's wrath on earth (1 Thessalonians 1:10; 5:9; Revelation 3:10; 6–19). The only similarities between this parable and the passages that teach the rapture are that (1) both involve a wedding motif; (2) the bridegroom's arrival time is unknown; and (3) both exhort believers to preparedness. But it does not follow that similarities between passages mean they are speaking of the same truths, doctrines, or events. Only a careful examination of verses *in their context* reveals the meaning of a given passage.

Finally, there are plenty of other passages in the New Testament that encourage believers to be ready for Jesus' return at the *rapture* (1 Peter 4:7; 5:8; 1 John 3:1-3; Revelation 3:2-3). However, Matthew 25:1-13 isn't one of them. We don't have to force an interpretation on the passage to justify our need to be prepared for the rapture, or to misconstrue and misapply Jesus' words to include the rapture in the Olivet Discourse. I understand Matthew 24–25 to be speaking to a different audience concerning a different period of time, and for a different return of Jesus Christ. However, within 36 hours of his sitdown discourse there on the Olivet hillside, Jesus *does* introduce, for the first time, the doctrine of the rapture. This occurred on Thursday evening in the upper room (John 14:1-3).

So if Christ isn't teaching his disciples about the rapture here, what, then, is the purpose of this end-times parable?

THE TWO RETURNS

As mentioned before, there *are* similarities between some aspects of the rapture and second coming. And to better understand both, let's take a look at the ancient Jewish betrothal custom Jesus uses to describe both events.

One of the most important Bible study skills is recognizing the challenges we face in accurately understanding and interpreting God's Word. Among those challenges are what I call the four gaps: chronological, linguistic, geographical, and cultural. In other words, our lives today are separated by a sort of "distance" from Scripture due to the fact it was written thousands of years ago, in three unfamiliar languages, in foreign lands, and in the context of different cultures and customs.

Of interest in this parable is the ancient Jewish people's cultural custom of betrothal and marriage.

Jewish Messianic scholar Dr. Arnold Fruchtenbaum, in his classic *Yeshua: The Life of Messiah from a Jewish Perspective*, outlines the four stages of a first-century Jewish wedding.

1. The "arrangement" corresponds when the Father "chose us in him before the foundation of the world" (Ephesians 1:4). The price was paid for us when Jesus died for our sins on the cross (1 Corinthians 6:20; Acts 20:28; 1 Corinthians 7:23; 1 Peter 1:18; Revelation 5:9).

2. The "fetching" of the bride occurs at the rapture, when Jesus will return in the air to take us to the Father's house (John 14:1-3; 1 Thessalonians 4:13-18).

3. The "ceremony" will take place in heaven while the 7-yr tribulation is happening on Earth (Revelation 19:7). Having been made perfect at the rapture (cleansed from the presence of sin and the sin nature) we will experience the completeness of our salvation at this time.

4. The "wedding feast" or supper will likely occur on earth during the millennial kingdom (Matthew 22:1-2; 25:10; Luke 14:15; Revelation 19:9).[2]

However, as we have discovered, though the illustration is similar, the application is not. Here in Matthew 25, we are at least seven years *past* the rapture, as Jesus' context is the close of the tribulation and his second coming. Second, the audience is Jewish believers, not church-age saints. So the timing and the participants are different. At his second coming, Christ will bring the church with him from heaven, where they have been while the events of the tribulation were unfolding on earth (Revelation 19:7-8, 14).

Though some see the virgins as representative of the Gentiles in the tribulation, the context suggests a more Jewish identification (we will look at the tribulation-era Gentiles' inclusion into the kingdom in chapter 17). This future kingdom concept is revealed throughout the Gospels as being *presented* to the Jews (Matthew 3:2; 4:17, 23; Luke 19:11-18), *rejected* by the Jews (Matthew 21:43; Luke 19:42-44; Acts 1:6), and then *re-offered* to the Jews (Matthew 25:1-10). Here in this parable, Jesus is giving his future Jewish brethren a major "pro tip" on how to be *ready* and *watchful* for his return.

GIVE ME OIL IN MY LAMP

The ten virgins (wedding attendants, bridesmaids) are divided into two categories: wise and foolish. Because the exact day and hour of the groom's arrival to claim his bride was unknown, and because the small lamps held a limited amount of oil, it would be prudent to have extra oil set aside to replenish the supply should the bridegroom delay his coming. And in those final days of the tribulation's second half, the Jews will long for the return of the Messiah. And so, they wait. And because he appears to delay his arrival, the prospect of Jesus coming will be mocked and ridiculed (2 Peter 3:3-7).

But why would the Lord appear to delay his Son's return? Why will he wait? I believe it's so that the rest of God's elect might come to repentance and faith in Jesus Christ (2 Peter 3:8-9).

God's patience in waiting for people to be saved will seem like a "delay," but from heaven's perspective, those days will actually be "cut short," or limited, in order to spare the lives of his saints from Antichrist's wrath (Matthew 24:22; Mark 13:20).

In this parable, when the bridegroom did not appear during the day and into the night, the virgins became drowsy and went to sleep. Unbeknownst to them, the bridegroom had decided to surprise his betrothed by coming at night: "At midnight there was a shout, 'Behold, the bridegroom! Come out to meet him'" (Matthew 25:6).

Startled, all ten virgins awoke and arose, quickly trimming the wicks of their lamps. However, five of them discovered they were out of oil (verses 7-8). Not wanting to be in the dark, they asked for oil from the others. "The foolish said to the prudent, 'Give us some of your oil, for our lamps are going out.' But the prudent answered, 'No, there will not be enough for us and you too; go instead to the dealers and buy some for yourselves'" (verses 8-9).

The five foolish virgins went looking to purchase oil, but because it was the middle of the night, none was to be found. Meanwhile, the five who were ready and prepared accompanied the bridegroom to the wedding feast.

Once they arrived, the door to the house was shut (verse 10). Forced to wait until perhaps just before daybreak to purchase oil, the five foolish virgins arrived late at the banquet and were refused entrance.

Though this may sound cruel or unfair, consider the following truths from both this parable and the prophetic Word. First, the wise virgins could not afford to give away their own oil, as that would have prevented them from joining the bridegroom and the wedding procession in the dead of the night. Second, Jesus already prophesied that the gospel of the kingdom "shall be preached in the whole world as a testimony to all the nations [including Israel], and then the end will come" (Matthew 24:14). This means the Jews represented by the five foolish virgins would also have been warned to be ready. They would have been alerted by the 144,000 (Revelation 7:4-8; 14:1-5) and the two witnesses (Revelation 11:3-13). Bottom line: They had already refused the offer of the kingdom, illustrated by their lack of preparedness—the lack of oil in their lamps.

According to Revelation 7:9-17, a vast multitude of Gentile and Jewish believers do respond to the gospel message during the early stages of the tribulation. However, we also know that only a remnant (one-third) of the Jews will ultimately trust in Messiah (Zechariah 13:8-9; Romans 11:25-26).

And what will be the Lord's response to these foolish Jews on that day when they realize it's too late? "Truly I say to you, I do not know you" (Matthew 25:12).

Those are chilling words. And they are eerily similar to what Jesus will say to counterfeit Christians on the day of judgment. They will claim to have prophesied in his name, "and in Your name cast out demons, and in Your name perform many miracles." But Jesus will declare to them, "I never knew you; depart from Me, you who practice lawlessness" (Matthew 7:22-23).

Thomas Hobbes, the seventeenth-century English philosopher, wrote, "Hell is truth seen too late."[3]

Applied here, this is the experience of the five foolish virgins, or the Jews who fail to respond to the gospel and the warnings about Messiah's second coming. This is why Jesus concluded the parable by saying, "Be on the alert then, for you do not know the day nor the hour" (Matthew 25:13).

The Greek word for "alert" here is the same word Jesus used repeatedly to exhort these same Olivet Discourse disciples (minus Andrew) in the Garden of Gethsemane hours before his crucifixion. Jesus had said, "Remain here and *keep watch* with Me...you men could not *keep watch* with Me for one hour? *Keep watching* and praying that you may not enter into temptation" (Matthew 26:38, 40-41).

It's also the same word the apostle Paul used to encourage us to "*be alert* and sober" so that we are personally prepared for the rapture (1 Thessalonians 5:6).

Christians now, as well as the Jews during the tribulation, are told to prepare for the coming of the Lord—for the rapture and the second coming. Both groups are exhorted to be awake.

So, be awake and be prepared, my friend.

That's more than good-life advice or an echo of the Boy Scout motto. It's a divine command, applicable to

- two appearances of our Lord—the rapture and the second coming, and
- two groups of people—Israel and the church. But for
- *one* reason: Jesus Christ is coming back.

Perhaps a moment of reflection is appropriate for us right now. And a prayer: "Lord, how can I better prepare myself for the rapture? How can I be more awake and watchful? Help me to not slumber and sleep in this critical hour of history and soon prophetic fulfillment. Help me to keep my lamp full, and to be *ready*."

CHAPTER 17

BE WISE WITH WHAT YOU'VE BEEN GIVEN

Matthew 25:14-30

I n J.R.R. Tolkien's fantasy classic Lord of the Rings series, there is a curious exchange between two principal characters—Gandalf, the protagonist and leader of the Fellowship of the Ring, and Frodo Baggins, a hobbit of the Shire.

"I wish it need not have happened in my time," said Frodo (speaking of the ring's discovery and the burden of him now possessing it).

"So do I," said Gandalf, "and so do all who live to see such times. But that is not for them to decide. All we have to decide is what to do with the time that is given us."[1]

Wise words.

FROM LITERARY FANTASY TO FUTURE FACT

Far more significant than evil Sauron and Mount Doom in the Land of Mordor is the coming Antichrist, Babylon, and the godless global government that will rule over humanity in the last days. And for believers on earth during the end times, a sobering and telling decision must be made. They will have to decide what to do with the little remaining time that is given them.

This principle is at the core of Jesus' message to his future disciples. For this reason, he relates a parable to help them contemplate the personal responsibility required for that time.

> It is just like a man about to go on a journey, who called his own slaves and entrusted his possessions to them. To one he gave five talents, to another, two, and to another, one, each according to his own ability; and he went on his journey. Immediately the one who had received the five talents went and traded with them, and gained five more talents. In the same manner the one who had received the two talents gained two more. But he who received the one talent went away, and dug a hole in the ground and hid his master's money (Matthew 25:14-18).

The word "it" in verse 14 refers back to "the kingdom of heaven" in verse 1, and particularly one's entrance into this kingdom and his rewards in it.

Christ describes these slaves who worked for their master. Prior to embarking on a long journey, the master entrusts a portion of his possessions to them. To one, he gives five talents, to a second, two talents, and to the last, a single talent. In the first-century Roman economy, a talent was a measure of weight—about 3,000 shekels in weight. Thus, a talent of gold would have been worth more than a talent of silver. The word translated "money" in verse 18 is the Greek word that means "silver."

John MacArthur writes, "The ancient Roman Empire had a banking system that was in many respects like those of modern times. The maximum loan rate was 12 percent simple interest, and the interest earned on deposits was probably half that rate."[2]

Using modern equivalents, a Jewish talent is estimated to be roughly half a million dollars in today's money.[3]

Based on this scale, we could estimate the amount allotted to each slave to be as follows:

Slave 1 = $2,610,000

Slave 2 = $1,044,000

Slave 3 = $522,000

Notice Jesus says the slaves were given the talents "each according to his own ability" (Matthew 25:15). In other words, the master did not expect the same bottom-line return on each of their investments. It wasn't equal amounts of money he was looking for, but equal amounts of obedience and responsibility.

However, not every slave exhibited the same level of responsibility.

> Immediately the one who had received the five talents went and traded with them, and gained five more talents. In the same manner the one who had received the two talents gained two more. But he who received the one talent went away, and dug a hole in the ground and hid his master's money (verses 16-18).

Notice that the first two slaves used their allotment to double the master's investment. In fact, they did it without hesitation ("immediately"). By contrast, the third slave went and dug a hole, hiding his master's money, or silver. To be fair, it was not unusual to hide valuables in that day by burying them in the ground (Matthew 13:44). The only problem was that's not what the master expected. The intention was that these "brokers" were to find ways to multiply the money given to them.

A LONG ABSENCE AND
AN UNEXPECTED RETURN

Jesus goes on the reveal the plot of this parable:

> Now after a long time the master of those slaves came and
> settled accounts with them. The one who had received
> the five talents came up and brought five more talents,
> saying, "Master, you entrusted five talents to me. See, I
> have gained five more talents." His master said to him,
> "Well done, good and faithful slave. You were faithful with
> a few things, I will put you in charge of many things; enter
> into the joy of your master."
>
> Also the one who had received the two talents came up
> and said, "Master, you entrusted two talents to me. See,
> I have gained two more talents." His master said to him,
> "Well done, good and faithful slave. You were faithful with
> a few things, I will put you in charge of many things;
> enter into the joy of your master" (Matthew 25:19-23).

Upon the master's return, the slaves are called to settle their accounts
with him. The first slave uses the resources given to him, taking full
advantage of his stewardship. The result is that both he and his master's talents achieve their full potential.

The second slave does the same. As a result, he receives overwhelming praise from the master. Both slaves are rewarded with increased
authority and responsibility over the master's affairs.

These two are called "good and faithful," perhaps the highest verbal accolades they could have received. Consequently, they are both
invited to "enter into the joy of your master" (verses 21, 23). The
word "joy" here is translated as such throughout the New Testament.
However, it primarily refers to extending *favor*, or to be favorably

disposed. Spiritually, the word carries for us the idea of *experiencing* joy—knowing we are favored by God. Think about this: What level of joy would you experience if you knew you had found favor with God? What level of contentment would you know if you had the pleasure of God's own joy in you? That's the "joy of [the] master" these steward-slaves received.

THE RECKONING OF REBUKE

The third slave, however, did not receive the same favor from the master.

> The one also who had received the one talent came up and said, "Master, I knew you to be a hard man, reaping where you did not sow and gathering where you scattered no seed. And I was afraid, and went away and hid your talent in the ground. See, you have what is yours."
>
> But his master answered and said to him, "You wicked, lazy slave, you knew that I reap where I did not sow and gather where I scattered no seed. Then you ought to have put my money in the bank, and on my arrival I would have received my money back with interest. Therefore take away the talent from him, and give it to the one who has the ten talents" (verses 24-28).

Wow.

This slave presented his report to the master, attempting to justify his lack of productivity on the character and reputation of the master. But his assumptions were flawed. Had he actually known his master (like the other two slaves), he would have understood what was expected of him. But instead of moving forward by faith, he allowed his fear to influence his actions. Because of this, instead of being called "good and faithful," the master declared him to be "wicked" and "lazy." His excuse of who he believed the master to be, coupled with his own fear, was merely a disguise masking his own laziness and lack of commitment to the master.

At the very least, instead of putting the money in the ground, he should have put it in the bank, where it would have earned up to about 6 percent interest. Instead, the talent earned nothing. This slave's fear and lack of faith paralyzed him, earning him no joy from his master, but instead, the master's anger and condemnation. The slave clearly did not take his master, nor his stewardship, seriously.

The master's judgment included stripping the slave of his stewardship and giving it to the first slave (verses 28-29). The unproductive slave was also condemned to a place of "outer darkness; in that place there will be weeping and gnashing of teeth" (verse 30). Elsewhere, similar words are used by Jesus to refer to hell (Matthew 8:12; 13:42; 22:13; 24:51; Luke 13:28). Translated: No faith = no work, and no work = no real relationship with the master.

THE APPLICATION

We've established from both the general and immediate contexts that Jesus' words are directed to those Jews living during the time of the great tribulation. So we can reasonably conclude that the two faithful slaves refer to believing Israel, while the worthless slave describes those who remain in unbelief at this time.

My former professor Dr. Dwight Pentecost summarized the parable as follows:

> Christ in this parable revealed that the nation Israel, which had been set aside as God's servant (Exodus 19:5-6), received a responsibility for which they were unanswerable. In the Old Testament Israel was designed to be God's light to the

Gentile world. The candelabra in the tabernacle was to be a perpetual reminder of Israel's function. Because Israel was faithless to that function, Isaiah promised that another Light would come to bring light to the Gentiles (Isa 60:1-3).

Christ came as the "true light" (John 1:9; 8:12). God will set apart Israel again during the Tribulation to be His light to the world (Rev 7:1-8).

When Christ comes the second time, the nation will be judged to determine individual faithfulness to that appointment. Faithfulness will indicate faith in the person of Christ. Those who prove themselves faithful will be accepted into His Kingdom, but those who are faithless will be excluded from His Kingdom.[4]

Generally speaking, this parable is one of faithfulness versus wasted opportunity—of making the most of what you have been given versus a timid, fearful approach toward the gospel and Messiah's second coming.

The virgins in the previous parable were urged to be ready through *waiting*. Then the slaves in this story were exhorted to be ready through *working*. In the words Jesus spoke to his disciples on that Wednesday afternoon, he stressed the unexpected nature of his return (Matthew 24:36, 42, 44, 50; 25:13). In those coming days, those Jews who are faithfully waiting and working will be received into Christ's 1,000-year millennial kingdom, while the unbelieving part of Israel will suffer judgment and be cast into hell.

"BUT WHAT ABOUT ME?"

Though this parable has a specific audience and time of history in mind, we cannot help but wonder if there is a secondary application to our lives today. I believe the answer is a definite yes.

There are at least six timeless principles we can draw from Jesus' words to his future Jewish brethren:

1. God gives each of us a measure of stewardship (time, talents, treasure, giftedness, relationships, ministry, influence, etc.). We must never compare our opportunities or abilities with those of another believer (Romans 12:3-6; 1 Corinthians 12:4-11). The number of "talents" we've been given doesn't matter. What matters is what we do with them. Having even a little talent of influence is no excuse not to use it.

2. Every Christian will be rewarded based on the measure of faith and faithfulness they exercise in wisely investing the stewardship entrusted to them (1 Corinthians 3:10-14).

3. Some believers will receive more rewards than others (1 Corinthians 3:14-15). In both the kingdom and in heaven, all believers will be equally perfect, but not equally rewarded.

4. Some Christians will receive few or next-to-zero rewards, though every believer will go to heaven based on Jesus' finished work on the cross (1 Corinthians 3:15; 4:5; 2 Corinthians 5:10).

5. Those who merely profess Christ—and who are given the opportunity to grow and be productive for Jesus—but do not bear any real fruit prove themselves to be counterfeit Christians, and thus will be excluded from heaven (Matthew 7:13-23; Luke 14:34-35). They are like the "wicked" and "lazy" slave in this parable.

6. We must combine our knowledge of God, biblical wisdom, and our love for him to help us maximize our time and resources during this life. Paul lived this way, which enabled him to say this, with confidence, at the end of his life:

I have fought the good fight, I have finished the course, I have kept the faith; in the future there is laid up for me the crown of righteousness, which the Lord, the righteous Judge, will award to me on that day; and not only to me, but also to all who have loved His appearing (2 Timothy 4:7-8).

Truly, Paul wasted nothing. He left it all on the playing field.

MY ONE SHOT

That's what you and I want to do as well. Occasionally, I hear someone remark concerning another believer, "He is so heavenly minded that he is no earthly good." But in my experience, I have rarely encountered such a Christian. I see much more the flip side—professing Christians who are so earthly minded that they are no heavenly good. In other words, their minds, money, skills, giftedness, influence, and opportunities are invested far more in temporary, earthly pursuits than in the things that impact eternity.

The late great C.T. Studd, a professional cricket player at Cambridge, set aside his athletic pursuits to become an evangelist and missionary. He penned a memorable poem, a portion of which reads,

> Two little lines I heard one day,
> Traveling along life's busy way;
> Bringing conviction to my heart,
> And from my mind would depart;
> Only one life, 'twill soon be past,
> Only what's done for Christ will last.
>
> Only one life, yes only one,
> Soon will its fleeting hours be done;
> Then, in "that day" my Lord to meet,

And stand before His judgment seat;
Only one life, 'twill soon be past,
Only what's done for Christ will last...

Give me Father, a purpose deep,
In joy or sorrow, Thy word to keep;
Faithful and true what e'er the strife,
Pleasing Thee in my daily life;
Only one life, 'twill soon be past,
Only what's done for Christ will last...

Only one life, yes only one,
Now let me say, "Thy will be done";
And when I'll hear the call,
I know I'll say "twas worth it all";
Only one life, 'twill soon be past,
Only what's done for Christ will last.[5]

Our Lord himself pictured this sense of purposeful urgency in John 9:4: "We must work the works of Him who sent Me as long as it is day; night is coming when no one can work."[6]

Another legendary professor of mine at Dallas Theological Seminary would often remind us that the greatest tragedy of all is a wasted life. Conversely, the greatest joy is a life lived to the fullest in fellowship and faithful service to our great God and Savior.

Make sure yours is the latter, so that you, too, will hear those words: "Well done, good and faithful slave. You were faithful with a few things, I will put you in charge of many things; enter into the joy of your master."

PART 5

HOW WILL IT ALL END?

CHAPTER 18

THE JUDGMENT OF THE GENTILES

Matthew 25:31-46

I heard the story of a man who visited his physician for his yearly checkup. Afterward, the doctor asked him to sit down to discuss the results.

"I have good news and bad news," the doctor announced.

"Oh?" the man responded. "Well, give me the good news first."

"The good news is that you have twenty-four hours to live," said the physician.

"Twenty-four hours?" the man retorted. "If that's the good news, then what's the bad news?"

The doctor said, "The bad news is, I should have told you that yesterday."

The Bible's prophecies regarding the last days contain both good news as well as bad. Unfortunately, some people won't discover the good news until it's too late. And this is one of the reasons the Bible is roughly one-third prophetic—to give us prior information, warning, and encouragement.

Throughout Scripture, God gives his people advance notices about what will occur in his divine narrative for Israel and the future of humanity. That's why I often call prophecy "a heads-up on history." In fact, so proactive is God that the very first prophecy in the Bible is found in its first book, and it concerns the ultimate defeat and end of evil found in the last book (Genesis 3:15; Romans 16:20; Revelation 20:10).

This prophetic thread woven all through Scripture is one way the Lord not only informs us of what's to come, but also prepares us to experience his prophetic plan (Titus 2:13; 1 John 3:1-3). And for those who will live through and endure the tribulation years, Jesus provides the prophetic teaching we find in Matthew 24–25, which concludes with this final parable we're about to study. And as it turns out, this parable also includes both good and bad news.

THE KINGDOM IS COMING

Describing his future return, Jesus declares, "When the Son of Man comes in His glory, and all the angels with Him, then He will sit on His glorious throne" (Matthew 25:31).

Christ is pointing the disciples back to his earlier words regarding his second coming (Matthew 24:29-31). Again, this climactic event will mark the conclusion of the seven-year period of divine judgment upon a post-rapture population. And we have already explored the "great glory" (verse 30) that will surround Jesus' epic return to planet Earth.

But by bringing this up in chapter 25, Jesus also answers a question that had been lingering in their minds—namely, when will "thy kingdom come" become a reality? (cf. Luke 19:11; 24:21; Acts 1:6). Long before, about 1,000 years prior to Christ, God promised a Jewish King David that one of his descendants would sit on his throne forever (2 Samuel 7:16). Then when the angel Gabriel visited Mary, he delivered the message that her child would be the eternal fulfillment of that Davidic prophecy, proclaiming,

Behold, you will conceive in your womb and bear a son, and you shall name Him Jesus. He will be great and will be called the Son of the Most High; and the Lord will give Him the throne of His father David; and He will reign over the house of Jacob forever, and His kingdom will have no end (Luke 1:31-33).

This throne, kingdom, and King Messiah was what the Jews had waited and longed for. Now Christ was revealing to his men the precise timing of the prophesied kingdom, and that his glorious appearing will lead to a "glorious throne" (millennial kingdom—Matthew 25:31).

THE VALLEY OF DECISION

But between the time of Jesus' return and the official inauguration of his kingdom, our Lord will have some unfinished business to tend to. The armies of the world will have just been annihilated at Armageddon, Bozrah, and around Jerusalem by the "sharp sword" coming from Jesus' mouth at the second coming (Revelation 19:15). During this campaign of Armageddon, the conquering Christ will merely speak a word, and all his enemies will be destroyed. Following this, who will still be left alive on earth? We know the Antichrist and false prophet will have been cast into the lake of fire, presumably as its first occupants (verse 20).

Those who remain will be gathered to Jerusalem and divided into two groups: Jews and Gentiles. The remnant Jews (Israel) will have already called on their Messiah to rescue and redeem them, and Jesus will save every one of them at his second coming. That leaves only the Gentiles.

Dr. Arnold Fruchtenbaum puts this chronology into perspective for us: "Daniel points out that there will be a 75-day interval between the end of the tribulation and the beginning of the Messianic Kingdom

(Daniel 12:11-13). During this interval, a number of things will occur, one of which will be the judgment of the Gentiles."[1]

This means the remaining people to be dealt with are the "nations," or those whom Scripture calls "the Gentiles."[2]

Every person who managed to survive the seal, trumpet, and bowl judgments will be brought by God to what the prophet Joel referred to as "the Valley of Jehoshaphat" (Joel 3:2). Scholars have debated the location of this valley, but since the fourth century AD, many have identified it as the Kidron Valley, which divides Jerusalem and the Temple Mount from the Mount of Olives. During my visit to Jerusalem, I carefully walked parts of the Kidron, imagining what it will be like when Jesus gathers the nations to judge them upon his return.

With the temple area high above, I could see how this lower-elevation area, which technically extends 20 miles south all the way to the Dead Sea, could hold the remaining people from the Gentile nations.

Joel also called this location "the valley of decision" (Joel 3:14). But it's not an altar call that takes place here, but rather, a throne verdict. Those in the valley made their decision during the tribulation. Now it's time for Jesus to make his decision as Judge.

Their decision will determine who will be called the sheep and who will be designated as goats (Matthew 25:32).

THE BLESSED AND THE DAMNED

At stake in this judgment is one's entrance into Jesus' millennial kingdom. Christ will begin by dividing the people—the sheep on his right and the goats on his left. The significance of this is that favor and honor are given to those on the right side of the throne (1 Kings 2:19; Psalm 110:1; Matthew 26:64; Acts 2:33; 7:55; Romans 8:34; 1 Peter 3:22; Hebrews 1:3; 12:1-2). This will mean the difference between acceptance and rejection, between privilege and punishment, between heaven and hell.

Christ the King will then invite those on his right, "Come you who are blessed of My Father, inherit the kingdom prepared for you from the foundation of the world" (Matthew 25:34). Jesus starts by mentioning their reward; then he explains how it came to them: "For I was hungry, and you gave Me something to eat; I was thirsty, and you gave Me something to drink; I was a stranger, and you invited Me in; naked, and you clothed Me; I was sick, and you visited Me; I was in prison, and you came to Me" (verses 35-36).

In response to Jesus' words, the righteous Gentiles will be puzzled, wondering when they ever saw the Lord hungry or thirsty or in prison (verses 37-39). "The King will answer and say to them, 'Truly I say to you, to the extent that you did it to one of these brothers of Mine, even the least of them, you did it to Me'" (verse 40).

Several questions naturally arise from these verses:

- Who are "these brothers of Mine"?

- Who are "the least of them"?

- Is this passage teaching salvation by works?

- Do these people become saved because of their kind and compassionate treatment of others?

Let's begin with the first question. Occasionally, I will hear these verses quoted as a motivation or justification to feed the homeless or to give money to street-corner beggars. And though the merits of doing such things are debatable, this is clearly not what Jesus has in mind here.

So who are "these brothers of Mine"? And who are "the least of them"? Some have suggested these phrases refer to *all* tribulation believers, Jews and Gentiles alike. Granted, Jesus does refer to all those who have been sanctified as being his "brethren" (Hebrews 2:11). However, the golden rule of Bible interpretation is always *context*. Though there certainly are, at times, overlapping theological truths from passage to passage, it's vital to observe how a word is used in the specific and immediate context of a passage, chapter, or book.

Though it's possible Jesus could be referring to all believers, it makes more sense to take "brethren" here as his Jewish brethren, particularly the 144,000 Jewish evangelists who will appear at the beginning of the tribulation (Revelation 7:1-8). The most compelling contextual reason for this is that the 144,000 are clearly distinguished during the tribulation from righteous Gentiles—i.e., those who minister kindness and aid to them (Matthew 25:35-36). This means they are likely Jews, and more specifically, the 144,000, because the rest of the Jewish remnant will have been hiding out at Bozrah (Petra) during the second half of the tribulation (Matthw 24:16-20; Revelation 12:6; cf. Isaiah 41:17-20; Micah 2:12). Further, only Matthew's Gospel (which has the most overt Jewish overtones) records this portion of the Olivet Discourse.

Because of the 144,000 evangelists' courageous proclamation of the gospel during Antichrist's tyrannical reign, they will become one of Satan's prime targets for persecution—including, but not limited to

- financial hardship, likely due to their refusal to take the beast's mark (666), which prevents them from participating in the global economy

- health and physical challenges—hunger, thirst, sickness, nakedness, loss of homes (verses 35-36)

- arrest and imprisonment (verse 36)—in an effort to choke out the preaching of the gospel, Antichrist's "gestapo" will take as many of the 144,000 off the streets as possible. Even so, he will not be allowed to execute any of them, for God has "sealed" or protected them (Revelation 7:4; 14:1).[3]

The only group of people who will be bold enough to reach out to and care for these persecuted Jewish men are Gentile believers who have come to faith at this time, many of them no doubt as a result of the Jewish men's preaching and witness. One can only imagine the depth of gratitude and relationship these new Gentile Christians will have for those Jews who have led them to faith in Jesus during such catastrophic, difficult times.

Even though many of these Jews will be caught, captured, and incarcerated, they will not be deterred from their labor for our Lord. They will persevere in ministry, and untold numbers of people will end up trusting Christ during the tribulation (Revelation 7:9-17).

RIGHTEOUSNESS VERSUS REWARD

The next and more challenging questions relating to this passage are these: Is Jesus teaching a works-based salvation here? Are the Gentiles being granted entrance into his kingdom based on their treatment of the 144,000? Are we saved by being nice to the Jewish people?

The short answer is no, primarily because that would flatly contradict the whole of Scripture. Salvation is by grace through faith, and *not* by works (John 3:16; Romans 10:9-10, 13; Acts 16:31; Ephesians 2:8-10). So why does Jesus picture their salvation this way?

Keep in mind that during the tribulation, the divide between believers and unbelievers will be both wide and obvious. Think of the hateful divisions we see in our culture today—political partisanship, racial divides, left versus right, liberal versus conservative, and godliness versus depravity. We face ideological, philosophical, and religious differences. Divisions over gender, the 1 percent versus the 99 percent, rural versus urban, and hot-button issues such as abortion, gay rights bathroom access for transgenders, climate alarmists versus climate deniers, and the list goes on and on. It's so acute today that it seems like we have become a society made up of enemies. Granted, some of the above-mentioned issues are worthy of doing battle over. But no one can deny that connected to all those divides is a simmering cauldron of human emotions at risk of boiling over in a moment's notice. The hatred, verbal attacks, and even acts of violence associated with these divisions are becoming more commonplace these days.

But nothing we are seeing today compares with the great divide that will exist during the tribulation between those who worship Antichrist and those who follow Jesus. The whole planet will turn its terrible wrath upon anyone who names the name of Christ, and that seething hatred will especially be directed against the 144,000 and the two witnesses.

With that as background, who on earth would dare to defy Antichrist and global peer pressure, and to stand side by side with these Jewish followers of Yeshua? Who would be willing to boldly align themselves with the persecuted Jewish remnant? And who would do so knowing that their own lives would be at great risk?

Only one group would dare such a thing—Christians. Specifically, Gentile believers. Therefore, it seems scripturally supportable to conclude that the reason they will minister to and provide aid to the persecuted 144,000 is because they themselves have already come to faith in Jesus Christ. Their righteous deeds done in service to the Jews will not be the *cause* of their salvation, but rather, the *proof* of it (James 2:26). Their saving faith is what will fuel their fervent service and ministry to their Jewish brethren.

Again, scripturally and theologically, salvation by grace through faith must, of necessity, come first, resulting in a righteous standing before God (Romans 5:1: Ephesians 2:8-9). Then after people have been declared righteous by him, their lives will demonstrate the reality of that righteousness through their good works (Ephesians 2:10; James 2:14-26). But here, those good works are directed toward those whose ancestry began with Abraham. It was to this man alone, a Hebrew, that God made a perpetual, unconditional promise: "I will bless those who bless you, and the one who curses you I will curse. And in you all the families of the earth will be blessed" (Genesis 12:3).

That promise has been binding upon individuals and nations from Abraham's day until now and will continue to be so until the end of the age.

Another reason we know the sheep on Jesus' right side are not admitted into the kingdom as a result of works is because, like all believers, both their salvation and their entrance into Jesus' future kingdom was "prepared…from the foundation of the world" (Matthew 25:34). God's eternal choice of those who would believe began long before any of us had demonstrated a single righteous deed (Ephesians 1:4; John 1:12-13; Romans 9:11-16).

Here in Jesus' words, we see a beautiful and epic display of this faith-works principle. Righteous Gentiles (who are on Antichrist's "Most Wanted List") think nothing of their reputation or safety for their own lives (Revelation 12:11). Instead, they lay it all on the line so that their future kingdom neighbors can have food, water, clothing, shelter, comfort, and companionship. It is this very display of Christian love and compassion that deeply touches the heart of our Savior, enough so to highlight and honor them in his end-times prophetic narrative.

Further, Jesus equates the way they treat these Jewish brethren to how they treat Christ himself. The Lord made a similar comparison when he confronted Saul (Paul) on the road to Damascus: "'Saul, Saul, why are you persecuting Me?' And he said, 'Who are you, Lord?' And He said, 'I am Jesus whom you are persecuting'" (Acts 9:4-5).

In that dramatic encounter, Jesus equated the persecution of Christians to persecuting the Lord himself. That's how closely identified we are with him. At the close of the tribulation, Jesus will make the same personal connection with his Jewish brethren.

Just one day later, on Thursday evening in the upper room, the Lord would instruct his disciples, "A new commandment I give to you, that you love one another, even as I have loved you, that you also love one another. By this all men will know that you are My disciples, if you have love for *one another*" (John 13:34-35). In other words, this is one way we prove we are true disciples of Christ.

Jesus' principle is applicable both then and now, and this will be a crucial and tangible mark of a person's salvation during earth's final days.

What we can conclude from Christ's words is that during the tribulation, one of the primary evidences of a Gentile person's salvation will be their ministry to the Jewish people. On the other hand, those who align themselves with Antichrist will hate the Jews, as he does, and will face entrance into another destiny and location—"away into eternal punishment" (Matthew 25:46). What we have here, then, is…

- one people—Gentiles
- two groups—sheep and goats
- two destinations—eternal life in God's kingdom and eternal punishment in hell

Even though Jesus' prophetic teaching applies directly to a future period of time and specific groups on earth during the tribulation, still, we can make several practical observations and application to our lives right now:

1. All people break down into one of two groups: saved or lost (sheep or goats). There is no middle ground with God. Jesus urges those who hear him to "enter through the narrow gate; for the gate is wide and the way is broad that leads to destruction, and there are many who enter through it. For the gate is small and the way is narrow that leads to life, and there are few who find it" (Matthew 7:13-14).

   We are all on either the broad way or the narrow way.

2. How we treat our fellow believers and minster to them today (including the Jewish people) is a strong indication of our spiritual condition (Genesis 12:3; John 13:35; Galatians 6:10; Hebrews 10:24-25; James 2:15-26). Our works do not save us. They cannot (Ephesians 2:8-10). But they do demonstrate evidence of genuine, saving faith (James 2:17-26).

3. The phrase "least of them" in Matthew 25:40 is not a generic reference to the poor, the homeless, or to refugees and illegals. Rather, it points to believing Jews (likely the 144,000) during the tribulation days. We could apply this principle to helping persecuted and suffering Christians in our day, but there are other Scripture passages that more accurately address that issue. And we should also help and bless individual Jews now, this side of the tribulation.

4. Not everyone will make it to heaven—only those who have trusted in Christ for salvation. The heretical doctrine known as universalism is embraced today by false teachers and those who have departed from the faith (called "apostasy" in 2 Thessalonians 2:3; cf. 1 Timothy 4:1-5; 2 Timothy 4:1-5). God will not, at the end of time, categorically forgive all the sins of mankind and allow everyone into his kingdom. On the contrary, for most people there is a "terrifying expectation of judgment and the fury of a fire which will consume the adversaries" (Hebrews 10:27).

Revelation makes it clear that the vast majority of humanity will end up condemned before God and face a Christless eternity filled with everlasting torment and damnation (Revelation 14:9-11; 20:11-15).

With these words concerning the judgment of the Gentiles, Jesus of Nazareth closes out his Olivet Discourse. His disciples—Peter, James, John, and Andrew—must have listened with wide-eyed wonder as the Author of history unfolded the prophetic events of the end of the world to them. And though they, like us, still did not know the exact timing for the fulfillment of these prophecies, they were, however convinced about the certainty of them. They knew that every word the Son of God spoke that day will, like all Bible prophecy, come to pass, literally and exactly as he spoke them.

The Gospel writers do not reveal the time of day at which Jesus concluded his teaching, but perhaps it was late afternoon. From where Jesus and the disciples sat on the Mount of Olives, they had a panoramic, almost bird's-eye view of the temple and Jerusalem. The sun may have been setting over the city, an apt metaphor for how history will grow darker during the tribulation. And yet, simultaneously, the light of revelation given by Jesus also portrays the great and glorious revealing of the Son of Man at his second coming.

As had been the custom each day that week, after Jesus finished speaking, he and his disciples no doubt began the short hike over the Mount of Olives to the little town of Bethany, where they would spend the night. At the same time, the chief priest and elders were busy plotting to arrest Jesus and have him executed.

This was sad, for there was something very special about his death they did not understand.

PART 6

HOW TO ESCAPE THE COMING APOCALYPSE

CHAPTER 19

JESUS OFFERS
THE WAY OUT

Matthew 26:1-2

C harles Dickens, in his classic *A Tale of Two Cities*, describes the era of the French Revolution this way:

> It was the best of times, it was the worst of times, it was the age of wisdom, it was the age of foolishness, it was the epoch of belief, it was the epoch of incredulity, it was the season of light, it was the season of darkness, it was the spring of hope, it was the winter of despair, we had everything before us, we had nothing before us, were all going to Heaven, we were all going the other way.[1]

In his poetic portrait of the age, Dickens juxtaposes cultural contrasts, brush-stroking what became a literary masterpiece that has stood the test of time.

The apostle John, carried along by the wind of the Holy Spirit, does much the same in his description of the seven-year period we call the tribulation, painting for us a portrait of future history marked by both global peace and world war, repentance and hardened hearts, divine protection and devilish persecution, earthly chaos and catastrophes contrasted with heavenly calm and comfort. It's an era of false Christs and faithful witnesses, fatal sword wounds and sealed evangelists, ferocious demons and flying angels. Earth will become a place where a single mark can damn you and a simple message can save you, where the love of many will grow cold but the love of One will reach untold millions. This will be a tragic era of apostasy side by side with a glorious era of mass revival. A day of retribution and a day of rescue.

Dickens's words could also appropriately be applied to those seven years as the "best of times" and "the worst of times." In fact, Jesus himself prophesied in his Olivet sermon that the latter half of that time would bring a "great tribulation, such as has not occurred since the beginning of the world until now, nor ever will" (Matthew 24:21).

Translated, it will be the most awful time in human history. And this sobering truth begs the question: Who would ever want to suffer through such a time? What person would ever wish that upon anyone, particularly himself? Knowing what we now know through Jesus' prophetic warnings, why would anyone willingly choose *this* as their future?

The question answers itself. No sane person ever would.

THE ROAD TO CALVARY

As soon as Christ finishes his discourse on the coming tribulation, he immediately pivots and turns his thoughts to a more immediate prophetic future: "You know that after two days the Passover is coming, and the Son of Man is to be handed over for crucifixion" (Matthew 26:2).

Crucifixion.

A concept and practice all but forgotten in our modern, digital age, this brutal form of capital punishment, though employed by the Romans, was not originally invented by them. Rather, it was conceived some 500 years before Christ by the Persians. It's reported that King Darius of Persia took 3,000 of his political adversaries and had them crucified in Babylon. The practice was later utilized by the Greeks and Carthaginians.

And while the Romans didn't invent crucifixion, they did perfect it. Author S. Michael Houdmann comments:

> Crucifixion was meant to inflict the maximum amount of shame and torture upon the victim. Roman crucifixions were carried out in public so that all who saw the horror would be deterred from crossing the Roman government. Crucifixion was so horrible that it was reserved for only the worst offenders.[2]

First, the convicted criminal was beaten or scourged (and in Jesus' case, both—John 19:1-3). Then, and again like Christ, he would be compelled to carry his own crossbeam to the crucifixion site. Criminals were stripped naked as a way of further publicly shaming them before others. Spikes were driven through the wrists, severing muscles and tendons, and sending unbearable pain through the sensitive nerve endings. After being lifted up, and after the crossbeam is attached to the other upright beam, the victim's legs are slightly bent upward and his feet penetrated with a large spike, nailing them into the rough-hewn wood.

Now the weight of his entire body is resting on those three nails. Desperate for relief, he attempts to lift himself up, but the pull on his wrists and the pressure on his feet causes unimaginable agony. He struggles to draw a breath, as his chest muscles cramp between the pull of his outstretched arms. Pushing up with his feet, he gasps in air, quickly falling back down due to the jolt of pain. This pulls on his wrists, creating a no-win scenario of living torture.

Gradually, the urge to breathe is measured by the pain it takes to inhale and exhale. Because some criminals lingered in this semi-conscious, death-like state for days, soldiers would break their legs with a hammer, preventing them from pushing up and catching one more breath (John 19:31-33). Therefore, most died from asphyxiation. John MacArthur offers these further comments,

> According to Josephus, after Herod the Great died in 1 BC, the Roman governor of Syria, Quinctilius Varus, crucified 2,000 men to quell an uprising. Josephus also says that Titus crucified so many people when he sacked Jerusalem in AD 70 that there was no wood left for crosses and no place left to set them up. By the time of Christ, Rome had already crucified more than 30,000 victims in and around Judea. So, crosses with dead or dying people hanging on them were a common sight around Jerusalem and a constant reminder of Roman brutality.[3]

All that to say, the disciples were *very* familiar with the ordeal of crucifixion. But this wasn't the first time Jesus had told them he would die in this way. Before traveling to Jerusalem for what would be his final week of ministry, he had forewarned them: "Behold, we are going up to Jerusalem; and the Son of Man will be delivered to the chief priests and scribes, and they will condemn Him to death, and hand Him over to the Gentiles to mock and scourge and crucify Him, and on the third day He will be raised up" (Matthew 20:17-19).[4]

BEHIND THE SCENES

Though the torture and brutality of crucifixion was unimaginably horrific, something even worse awaited the Lord in just a few days. What the disciples did not yet fully understand was that, while their master was on the cross, an invisible transaction would take place. The Father, Son, and Spirit had pre-decided the manner of Jesus' death (crucifixion), but the real story of the cross was what would happen in the spiritual realm while he hung there. Jesus himself, in the moments before his arrest in the Garden of Gethsemane, contemplated the awful fate that awaited him. As he did so, he remarked to Peter, James, and John, "'My soul is deeply grieved to the point of death; remain here and keep watch with Me.' And he went a little beyond them, and fell on his face and prayed, saying, 'My Father, if it is possible, let this cup pass from Me; yet not as I will, but as You will'" (Matthew 26:38-39).

When Jesus returned, he found his disciples asleep. He spoke to Peter, then "He went away again a second time and prayed, saying, 'My Father, if this cannot pass away unless I drink it, Your will be done'" (verse 42).

The "cup" Jesus spoke of here represented his payment for the sins of the world. And why was that such a big deal?

Because it meant he would suffer what those currently in hell are suffering—condemnation, separation, and damnation—all part of the judgment due every sinner who has ever lived.

Part of the penalty of being sinners is that we are already under the condemning sentence of God's judgment (John 3:18, 36; Ephesians 2:1-2). We are spiritually separated from a relationship with God (Ephesians 2:12) and marked for eternal punishment (Romans 6:23). In Scripture, "death" always means "separation"—when a person dies, his spirit is separated from his body (2 Corinthians 5:8).

Similarly, having been conceived as sinful humans (Psalms 51:5; 58:3), we are born spiritually dead, or separated from the life of God (Ephesians 4:18).

A person may spend his entire life in this separated state or condition. But that isn't the end of the story. Because God is holy and righteous, his nature and character demands that every sin be punished or paid for. And the punishment is administered in a place called hell, a place of eternal fire (Matthew 25:41).[5]

The Bible states that ultimately, a place called the lake of fire will house all unrepentant, unredeemed sinners (Revelation 20:14). It is a place of unrelenting, unending torture of body and soul day and night, 24/7. A place where there is not the slightest second of reprieve or relief, but rather, "the smoke of their torment goes up forever and ever; and they have no rest day and night" (Revelation 14:11).

Just how bad is this pain and torment? One of the angels in Revelation explains, "He will also drink of the wine of the wrath of God, which is mixed in *full strength* in the *cup of His anger*; and He will be *tormented with fire and brimstone*" (verse 10).

The word "cup" here is not only the same Greek word Jesus used when he prayed in the Garden of Gethsemane (Greek *poterion* = wine cup), it also symbolizes the same wrath of God poured out at the cross on Jesus. The unsaved will suffer this wrath eternally in the afterlife.

Contrary to religious folklore, the devil is not in charge of hell. Instead, he and his fallen angels will themselves experience their own level of unrelenting torment (Matthew 25:41; Revelation 20:10).

The truth is that the one presiding over hell and the lake of fire is God himself. Those who dwell there experience God's holy anger and wrath against sin "in the presence of the holy angels and in the presence of the Lamb" (Revelation 14:10).

This is the kind of wrath God exercises against sin. This is the justice God reserves for anyone who is a sinner. Because he is righteous, he must treat such people as if they *are* sin.

Translated: This divine wrath is what Jesus Christ experienced while he hung on the cross. Paul, writing under the inspiration of the Holy Spirit, put it this way: "He made Him who knew no sin to be sin on our behalf, that we might become the righteous of God in Him" (2 Corinthians 5:21).

When we say, "Jesus died in our place for our sins," we mean that

God the Father took all the punishment, wrath, and torment of eternity against our sin and laid it on Christ at the cross. Romans 5:8 proclaims, "God demonstrates His own love toward us, in that while we were yet sinners, Christ died for us."

That's right. His death involved a double-barrel damnation.

Jesus took the full wrath *of* God, while simultaneously experiencing a tormenting separation *from* God.

But why? After all, we know he didn't have to. Nothing about us inherently obligates the triune God to do anything other than condemn, abandon, and punish us, for this is exactly what we deserve (John 3:18, 36; Romans 3:10-12).

So why did he do it? In a word, love. He suffered because he loves us (John 3:16; 15:13; Romans 5:8). Because he loves *you.*

Pause a moment to marvel at that reality.

Jesus went to the cross because he desired to save you and me from the penalty of our sin (Romans 5:8; Hebrews 7:26-27; 1 Peter 3:18). Again, not because he was under obligation. But because it pleased him to do so.

This Jesus of Nazareth was willing to endure something he had never, in eternity, known—a break in his relationship with the Father. This is why, while on the cross, he cried out, "Eli, Eli, lama sabachthani?" That is, "My God, My God, why have You *forsaken Me?*" (Matthew 27:46).

While upon the cross, the God-man Jesus Christ (100 percent God, 100 percent man) simultaneously suffered total abandonment from the Father and absorbed the full fury of his wrath toward sin. We may never fully comprehend the depth of the sacrifice Jesus made to deliver us from sin's penalty, power, and presence, but this we can say: Who would or could do such a thing for undeserving sinners like you and me? Answer: only an eternal, all-powerful God who loves you more than you could ever imagine.

No one will ever love you like Jesus does. No level of love on this planet or in this life could ever mirror the matchless love Jesus Christ has for you. And nothing you do could ever persuade God to love you any more or any less than he did on that dark Friday morning in AD 33.

Let me say it again. No sin you have ever committed or will commit can diminish that love. And no good thing you have ever done can increase it. That's because God's love is not dependent upon the object of his love, but rather, upon himself and who he is.

In short, *he* loves you because *he* is good, not because *you* are. He loves you because he is love, not because you are lovely or lovable.

It might be worth 60 seconds for you to reread the previous paragraph and take time to reflect on it.

WHAT'S LEFT TO DO?

At the cross, a colossal collision took place. There, righteousness met depravity, and redemption clashed with retribution. At Calvary, wrath was poured out alongside grace. Justice is satisfied and mercy is supplied. It's where we are brought near to God. No longer enemies, we become friends—children of the Father (Ephesians 1:4-5; 1 John 3:1-3).

This is why Paul wrote, "In Him we have redemption through His blood, the forgiveness of our trespasses, according to the riches of His grace, which He lavished on us" (Ephesians 1:7-8).

All that left for us to do is to "*believe* in the Lord Jesus," and be saved (Acts 16:31).

To believe signifies more than intellectually agreeing with the facts presented in Scripture. The biblical word means "to trust in, cling to, and rely on." True, saving faith is a full dependence upon the Lord Jesus Christ and his finished work on the cross. It's trusting him to do for you what you could never do for yourself—namely, to

- cleanse and forgive you of your sin (Colossians 1:14)

- reconcile you into a right relationship with God (Romans 5:10-11)

- make you a child of God, adopting you into his family (John 1:12; Romans 8:14-16; Ephesians 1:4-5)

- make you an heir of God and joint heirs with Christ (Romans 8:17)

- provide for you a guaranteed home in heaven (John 14:1-3)

- give you peace *with* God and the peace *of* God (Philippians 4:6-8)

- give you true joy (John 15:11)

- cause you to experience the ongoing love and life God provides (John 10:10; Ecclesiastes 2:25)

- guarantee your rescue from the awful seven-year tribulation (1 Thessalonians 1:10; 5:9; Revelation 3:10)

The gospel of Jesus is *the* only deliverance from spiritual misery—now, during the tribulation, and for all eternity.

Do we still suffer hardships in this life as believers? Absolutely. Problems, pains, and even persecution may come our way. But no suffering we experience now remotely compares to the reward and glory the Lord will one day give us when we are with him (Romans 8:18).

So, dear reader, may I ask:

- Do you know this Jesus of Nazareth?

- Is he your personal Savior?

- Have you trusted in him as your only hope of salvation, both in this life and the next?

- Are you 100 percent certain that if you died today, you would spend eternity with Jesus?

Because Christ has already warned us what kind of future awaits planet Earth during the tribulation, and because we've come to know that he alone is qualified to make such prophecies, doesn't it make sense to accept his gracious offer of salvation and deliverance from that awful era?

Jesus is your *way out*.

CHAPTER 20

JESUS RESCUES HIS BRIDE FROM THE COMING WRATH

John 14:1-3

We have already learned that in Jesus' long teaching on the end times, there is no mention of the rapture. Why not? If it is truly the next prophetic event on God's calendar (and the one that concludes the church age), why not mention it? This is easily understood when we consider the following:

1. The Olivet Discourse (Matthew 24–25) flowed out of the disciples' question regarding Jesus' prophecy about the Jewish temple (Matthew 24:1-3). Jesus then proceeded to tell them about the coming destruction of that temple (Matthew 24:2; Mark 13:2; Luke 21:6) and of Jerusalem itself, which occurred in AD 70 (Luke 21:20-24). In the mind of a first-century Jew, the destruction of the temple and the second coming of Messiah (which will end the present age and usher in the kingdom age) went together (Zechariah 14:1-11). The disciples didn't even know to ask about the church or the

rapture, two mysteries that were to later be revealed. They were only concerned about the temple, Israel, Jerusalem, Messiah's coming, and his future kingdom.

Their initial inquiry in Matthew 24:3, which launched the entire Olivet Discourse, consisted of questions asked *by* Jews about *Jewish* religion and *Jewish* prophecies that required a *Jewish* response concerning the future of the *Jewish* people. Therefore, there was no need to mention the rapture...yet.

2. The setting of Jesus' words in Matthew 24–25 is the future tribulation period. This is known in Scripture as the "time of Jacob's trouble," which will occur after God restores the people of Judah and Israel back to the land he had promised to their ancestors (Jeremiah 30:3-4, 7 NKJV). One of the primary purposes of this seven-year time span is to restore Israel spiritually (Jeremiah 30:22; Hosea 6:1-2; Zechariah 12:10). Again, the focus of the text is Israel, not the church.

3. The concept of the church was still relatively foreign to the minds of the disciples at this point. In fact, Christ had used the word only two times previously (Matthew 16:18; 18:17).

Technically, the life and ministry of Jesus took place during the Old Testament, or under the old covenant. It wasn't until Passover was observed in the upper room that Christ introduced his new covenant (Luke 22:19-22). And this covenant wasn't officially ratified until he paid for our sins on the cross.

Until Acts 2, the church was a nonexistent entity, having never been mentioned in the Old Testament. So to say that the rapture isn't a reality because its not mentioned in Jesus' Olivet Discourse is the equivalent of saying that the church isn't a reality because it's not mentioned in the Old Testament.

This takes us back to the concept of progressive revelation, or how God gradually communicated his truth over time. He didn't reveal everything at once, but in stages and theme by theme. A Jewish mind could not have comprehended the concept of a Jewish-Gentile church (separate from the synagogue and the Jewish faith). Again, this is why Paul referred to the church as a mystery—that believing Jews and Gentiles would form a new entity together (Ephesians 3:3, 6, 8-9; Colossians 1:25-26).

4. The rapture is only for Christians (believing Jews and Gentiles) and does not involve the nation of Israel, which has been under a divine "partial hardening" during the church age (Romans 11:25-26).

   Therefore, Jesus had no reason to mention the rapture to his disciples that afternoon on the Mount of Olives. It simply wasn't relevant to the questions they had asked him. It would be like a college student asking his professor about the final exam but then wondering why the professor didn't also include in his answer information about all tests that will be given prior to the final exam. The question was about the final, not an unknown number of tests and quizzes given beforehand.

5. As we will see, Jesus *does* address the rapture on the night before he is crucified. But the context of that setting is newer revelation about the new covenant in his blood, so it made more sense to teach them about the rapture at that time, not before.

In summary, people try to find the rapture in the Olivet Discourse because they simply want it to be there. This flows from several interpretive mistakes:

1. We (Western, modern Christians) desperately want to read ourselves into biblical passages, including ones that are not directed toward church-age believers.

2. We mistakenly equate Israel with the church (and vice versa), and view Jesus' disciples as representing the church in the Gospels.

3. Because we see Israel as being on the "back burner" for now, spiritually speaking (Romans 11:25-26), we thus attempt to interpret and apply all Israel-based passages of Scripture to us instead.

4. We assume the ones "taken" in Matthew 24:40-41 are Christians at the rapture.

5. We assume the ten virgins in Matthew 25 are Christians because a wedding motif is used there. But as we have seen, half of those virgins are rejected by Christ at the wedding ceremony and thus cannot be representing believers. Plus, they are bridesmaids, not the bride herself, so the application to the church breaks down.

It's like Jesus is saying to us, "I realize you want to know about the rapture, and I will get to that. But first, let me address my Jewish brethren about their role during the last days, okay?"

Having said all this, I do see many great and relevant principles we can apply from the Olivet Discourse.

For example, the signs of the tribulation—deception, false teachers, counterfeit Christs, wars and rumors of wars, persecution, lawlessness, the spirit of antichrist, antisemitism—are all presently emerging and converging with greater velocity in our day.

The calls to be watchful, ready, and prepared for the second coming of Christ also applies to our anticipation of the rapture, though there are plenty of other New Testament passages and verses that speak directly to that subject.

The fact that, during the tribulation, the gospel will be preached "in the whole world" (Matthew 24:14) ought to motivate us now to help fulfill the Great Commission as much as possible this side of the rapture (Matthew 28:18-20). We do this not because we *have* to reach the whole world in order for the rapture to occur, but because Jesus commanded us to go into all the world and make disciples.

LAST SUPPER, LAST WORDS

The day after Jesus taught his Olivet Discourse (Thursday), he gathered with his disciples for one last meal. John describes the scene this way: "Now before the Feast of the Passover, Jesus knowing that His hour had come that He would depart out of this world to the Father, having loved His own who were in the world, He loved them to the end" (John 13:1).

Are there any more tender words written than these?

During this final meal, Jesus washes the feet of the Twelve, teaching them by example to serve one another going forward (verses 5-17). He then speaks of his betrayal by one of the disciples; Judas Iscariot had already been influenced by the devil to do this (verse 2). Satan possessed Judas, proving he had never genuinely put faith in Christ to begin with (verse 27; cf. Matthew 26:24; Mark 14:21; Acts 1:16-19, 25).

Jesus then turns to another subject—that of his death and departure from the disciples. As he does, he reveals something about his future as well as theirs. Knowing that the reality of him leaving would cause immediate sorrow, Jesus comforts them with a unique and simple promise:

> Do not let your heart be troubled; believe in God, believe also in Me. In My Father's house are many dwelling places; if it were not so, I would have told you; for I go to prepare a place for you. If I go and prepare a place for you, I will come again and receive you to Myself, that where I am, there you may be also (John 14:1-3).

These are the first recorded words of Jesus concerning the rapture. Let's take a fresh and careful look at them through the eyes and minds of those who were in the upper room that Thursday night. They didn't yet have Paul's teaching on the subject, nor did they know to call it "the blessed hope" (Titus 2:13). All they knew was what Jesus said, and the entirety of their rapture knowledge was densely packed into just three verses.

Interestingly, Jesus first gives the disciples the application to their lives before he explains the rapture itself. He gives them three commands: (1) Don't allow your heart to be troubled (due to my soon departure). (2) Believe in God (continue to believe), and (3) believe also in me (because I *am* God).

The word "troubled" here means "to set something in motion that needs to be still." It is used elsewhere in the Gospels to refer to someone being mentally or emotionally unsettled or terrified (Matthew 2:3; 14:26; Mark 6:50; Luke 24:38). John used the word to describe how an angel "stirred" the waters of a pool (John 5:4, 7).

Paul would later use this word to describe how false teachers in the Galatian church were "disturbing" the faith of believers there by teaching another gospel (Galatians 1:7; 5:10). It carries the idea of being restless, anxious, and upset. You've felt that before, haven't you?

"Don't worry," Jesus comforts them. "Keep believing in God and in me."

So that's what they are to do. But why? Why should their hearts be filled with peace instead of anxiety, and why should they keep putting their faith in him and the Father? Jesus gives them four rock-solid reasons:

1. The Father has a big house.

Jesus assures them that heaven is real, and that there is plenty of room there for all who put their faith in him. Rather than the concept of heaven simply being an altered state of mind or being, Christ wants them to know that it is an actual place where believers will dwell. He tells them it is eternal and secure because it is the Father's house.

2. Jesus will return for his disciples one day.

As a pastor for more than three decades, I officiated many funerals of believers. One truth I was always careful to declare was that, for Christians, we never say, "Goodbye," but rather, "Until we meet again." This is what Jesus is telling us here. Notice he says "if" I go away, I "will" come again. We know that Jesus did indeed go away when he ascended from that very same Mount of Olives in Acts 1:9-11. And because he has shown himself to be God via his life, death, and resurrection, we know that he will make good on his promise to come again.

"But," some may ask, "could he here be referring to his second coming at the end of the tribulation? I mean, wasn't that what he had been teaching them about just one day earlier?"

It is true that the tribulation and second coming were the themes of the Olivet Discourse, but the rapture and the second coming cannot be the same event, for the following 19 reasons:

AT THE RAPTURE

1. Jesus comes in the air (1 Thessalonians 4:16-17)

2. Jesus comes for the church (1 Thessalonians 4:13-17)

3. Jesus returns to rescue us from the tribulation wrath to come (1 Thessalonians 1:10; 5:9; Revelation 3:10)

4. Believers are changed (1 Corinthians 15:51-53; 1 Thessalonians 4:17)

5. A signless event

6. Saints go to heaven (1 Thessalonians 4:17)

7. Not prophesied in the Old Testament

8. Affects only believers directly (1 Thessalonians 4:16-17)

9. Only believers will see Jesus (1 John 3:2)

10. Tribulation will begin afterward (1 Thessalonians 1:10; 5:9; Revelation 3:10)

11. No mention of Satan

12. Officially concludes the church age

13. Raises the dead in Christ from the grave (1 Thessalonians 4:16-17)

14. Bride is called to a wedding

15. Afterward, Antichrist is revealed and reigns (2 Thessalonians 2:6-8; Revelation 6:1-2)

16. Occurs in an instant (1 Corinthians 15:51-52)

17. Church saints rewarded afterward (1 Corinthians 4:5; 2 Corinthians 5:10)

18. Jesus returns to heaven afterward (1 Thessalonians 4:17)

19. Believers removed, only unbelievers remain behind (1 Thessalonians 4:13-17)

AT THE SECOND COMING

1. Jesus comes to earth (Zechariah 14:4)

2. Jesus returns with his church (Revelation 19:14)

3. Jesus returns to bring wrath on his enemies (Revelation 19:11-16)

4. Believers already changed (Revelation 19:7-8)

5. Preceded by many signs (Matthew 24)

6. Saints come from heaven to earth (Revelation 19:14)

7. Prophesied in the Old Testament (Daniel 2:44-45; 7:9-14; 12:1-3; Zechariah 12:10; 14:1-15)

8. Affects all men on earth (Revelation 19:15, 18)

9. Every eye will see him (Revelation 1:7)

10. Millennial kingdom begins afterward (Revelation 20:1-9)

11. Satan bound for 1,000 years (Revelation 20:1-3)

12. Officially concludes the tribulation

13. Puts the unrighteous in the grave (Isaiah 63:1, 3-4; Revelation 14:19-20; 19:13-15)

14. Birds are called to a feast (Revelation 19:17-19)

15. Afterward, Antichrist is thrown alive into the lake of fire (Revelation 19:20)

16. Involves a battle campaign lasting perhaps a day (Isaiah 63:1-4; Zechariah 14:4)

17. Tribulation saints rewarded afterward (Revelation 20:4)

18. Jesus stays on earth afterward (Revelation 3:21; 5:10; 20:4, 6, 9)

19. Unbelievers removed, only believers remain (Matthew 24:39-41; Revelation 20:4)

3. Jesus is going to the Father's house "to prepare a place" especially for them.

Jesus is not returning to heaven to be idle, but rather, to be busy. The word "prepare" means "to make ready," like a meal that is fully prepared, similar to the Passover meal they had just eaten that had been prepared and made ready to serve (Matthew 26:17-19).

"Prepare" is also used to refer to Jesus' bride, who has "made herself ready" for "the marriage of the Lamb" (Revelation 19:7).

And finally, this word is used to describe the New Jerusalem "coming down out of heaven from God, *made ready* as a bride adorned for her husband" (Revelation 21:2). This is a compelling reason to equate "the Father's house" with the New Jerusalem. All this gives us a better sense of what Jesus meant when he said he is preparing individual places for us in heaven.

Based on the dimensions of the New Jerusalem as given in Revelation 21:16, Bible scholar Ron Rhodes writes,

> Someone calculated that if this structure is cube-shaped, it would allow for 20 billion residents, each having his or her own private 75-acre cube. If each resident were smaller, the city would have room to accommodate one hundred thousand billion people with plenty of room left over for parks, streets, and other things you would see in any normal city.[1]

The Father's house will surely be creative, beautiful, amazing, and full of life—just like God. And with plenty of room for all!

And there's one more reason the disciples (and us) should be free from worry and fear:

4. Jesus guarantees we will be with him forever.

Heaven is a real place. But the very essence of heaven is not the place itself, but the *person.* Heaven is being with God himself. That's because, at its core, Christianity is all about a relationship with our Creator, Savior, and Lord. What God wants is for us to be with him. This is a theme we see repeated throughout the New Testament (Mark 3:14; John 17:24; Philippians 1:23; Revelation 17:14).

During Jesus' last night with his disciples, he spoke a sacred promise to them about his return. And though he has yet to fulfill that rapture promise, we can be assured of its reliability based on his proven, trustworthy character. That's why he is described in Revelation 1:5 and 3:14 as "the faithful witness" and "the faithful and true Witness."

As we have learned, there is a direct parallel between the Jewish wedding customs of the day and the doctrine about the rapture. Jesus beautifully portrayed his relationship to his bride as a divine romance, birthed in the very heart of God (Ephesians 1:4-5).

Presently, we are in the betrothal period, and we await the day when our Bridegroom will return, unannounced, to snatch us up and carry us away to the Father's house. This is the essential meaning of the Greek word *harpazo* (1 Thessalonians 4:17)—"to seize, snatch away, carry off by force." It is what a bridegroom would do for his bride. And it is exactly what Jesus will do for us when he returns.

And why do we call this event the rapture? It goes back to that word *harpazo*. Jerome, a fourth-century church father, one of the greatest Christian scholars of his day, spent three decades producing a Latin version of the Scriptures that would become the standard for the next 1,000 years. When he translated *harpazo* from Greek to Latin, he used the word *rapiemur*, a form of the verb *rapio*. The English word *rapture* was eventually used to describe this glorious event. *Rapture* is simply a transliteration (or English version) of the Latin *rapturo*.

Because we know the rapture and the second coming cannot be the same event, we must then ask *when* the rapture will occur in relationship to the second coming. We know from Revelation 19 that Jesus' second coming will occur at the close of the seven-year tribulation. So when will the rapture occur?

We could spend several chapters explaining the views and reasons related to the timing of the rapture. Suffice it to say there are three main views related to the rapture and the tribulation period:

1. The pre-trib rapture view

2. The mid-trib rapture view

3. The post-trib rapture view

Let's work our way backward, briefly unpacking each one.

The post-trib view has Jesus rapturing his church at the second coming, or just prior to it. We go up, then we come right back down. For me, this view is untenable for the following reasons:

- It allows no time between the rapture and second coming for the *bema*, or judgment seat of Christ (1 Corinthians 3:11-15; 2 Corinthians 5:10)

- It can't explain why the church is pictured early on in Revelation as being in heaven, before the tribulation begins (Revelation 4:4-11)

- If a post-tribulation rapture were true, then there is no need for the sheep and goats judgment (Matthew 25:31-46), and all believers at this point would simply be taken up to meet Jesus, not be left on earth to be told they were going into the kingdom

- At the second coming, believers are described as coming *from* heaven, not being taken up *to* it

- There is no mention of a rapture or any of its components (dead in Christ rising, meeting in the air, etc.) at the close of the tribulation—nothing resembling the

rapture of the bride takes place in Matthew 24–25 or
Revelation 19–20

- There is no judgment of unbelievers at the rapture (like
we see at the second coming in Matthew 25:31-46)

- Children will be born from mortal believers during the
millennial kingdom—this would be impossible if all
believers are raptured and transformed into their glorified bodies at the end of the tribulation (Isaiah 65:20)

For these reasons, I cannot entertain the post-trib view.

The mid-trib view sees Jesus' rapture as occurring three-and-a-half
years into the tribulation, at the time of Antichrist's abomination of
desolation. Those who hold to this view agree that we are raptured
prior to God's wrath being poured out during the tribulation. However, they claim it is not until the midpoint of the tribulation that
God begins to exhibit his wrath. This view has the church being rescued immediately prior to the abomination of desolation and Antichrist's mark of the beast.

One of the chief reasons I reject this view is because Revelation
6:1 clearly and unquestionably states that "the Lamb broke one of
the seven seals," thus inaugurating God's judgment protocol of the
seal, trumpet, and bowl judgments. According to this verse, God's
wrath begins at the *start* of the tribulation, not the middle (cf. Revelation 6:15-17).

Another reason this view doesn't hold water is because Scripture
portrays the rapture as a signless, imminent event. This means there
are zero signs leading up to it (this also eliminates the post-trib view,
which sees seven years of continuous signs prior to the rapture). Imminency also means that the rapture cannot be predicted. Yet with the
mid-trib view, the timing of the rapture *can* be forecast. One could
simply count the days from the signing of Antichrist's peace treaty

with Israel to the time when he suffers a fatal head wound, comes back from the dead, and enters the Jewish temple. That's your rapture date. However, this denies the doctrine of imminency. Because Scripture clearly states no one can know the timing of the Bridegroom's return, I reject this view.

The pre-trib view (the one I hold) believes the wrath of God begins at the very start of the tribulation. Because the Bible says the bride of Christ will be delivered by him from the wrath to come, and that God has not destined us for wrath but for obtaining salvation through our Lord Jesus Christ, we will not suffer *any* wrath from God (1 Thessalonians 1:10; 5:9; Revelation 3:10). Furthermore, all of the Father's righteous fury was exhausted on Jesus at the cross. "Therefore there is now no condemnation for those who are in Christ Jesus" (Romans 8:1).

Though one's belief regarding the timing of the rapture does not affect our salvation, and it shouldn't cause angry divisions in the body of Christ, it is nevertheless an important matter because the timing of the rapture determines whether or not church-age believers will suffer through unimaginable divine judgments, Antichrist's tyranny, the wrath of the false prophet, the mark of the beast, persecution, and almost-certain martyrdom. For that reason alone the timing of the rapture is worth your study.

Plus, there cannot be more than one rapture. That means only one of these three views is correct.

If you believe the Bible, you have to believe in a rapture. The question is *when* it occurs. This is an important doctrine that you should study for yourself.

I believe Jesus made it clear that he will return at some point in time, unexpectedly, to snatch up his bride and take her to the Father's house.

From the rest of the New Testament, it is also evident that the rapture and the second coming are two distinct events, separated by seven years from one another.

And what is our response to this promised rapture?
The Holy Spirit urges us to

- anticipate it (Romans 13:11-12)

- eagerly await it (1 Corinthians 1:7; Hebrews 9:28)

- long for it (1 Corinthians 16:22)

- look for it (Titus 2:13)

- wait for it (1 Thessalonians 1:10)

- fix our hope on it (1 Peter 1:13)

- know that it is imminent (1 John 2:18)

- encourage one another as we see the day approaching
  (Hebrews 10:25)

Why would God tell us to do these things and have this perspective if the rapture were a minor doctrine or optional truth?

THE END...BUT NOT THE END

Yes, the end of the world will come, literally and exactly as Jesus of Nazareth prophesied 2,000 years ago. And as we pay attention to what's going on globally, those prophecies are converging at an ever-expanding, ever-accelerating pace.

We cannot change or alter God's future prophetic narrative. But what we *can* do is to decide how we will live in light of it. Paul put it this way:

> Do this, knowing the time, that it is already the hour for you to awaken from sleep; for now salvation is nearer to us than when we believed. The night is almost gone, and the day is near. Therefore let us lay aside the deeds of darkness

and put on the armor of light. Let us behave properly as in the day, not in carousing and drunkenness, not in sexual promiscuity and sensuality, not in strife and jealousy. But put on the Lord Jesus Christ, and make no provision for the flesh in regard to its lusts (Romans 13:11-14).

In 1914, famed British explorer Sir Earnest Shackleton reportedly placed an advertisement in a London newspaper. It read,

> Men wanted for hazardous journey.
> Long hours, bitter cold, months without light,
> safe return doubtful.
> Reward in case of success.

The response to Shackleton's call was overwhelming. Hundreds applied, each one hoping they might have the chance to accompany the knighted explorer. Joining him meant they would become the first to cross the Antarctic continent on foot, a chance to write themselves into the history books. After personally interviewing the applicants, Sir Earnest settled on a crew of 27 men, each one of them a specialist in his own area of expertise. There were doctors, cooks, carpenters, and seasoned seamen, all filled with anticipation upon accompanying Shackleton on the great voyage.

Sailing to Antarctica, the *Endurance* soon became stuck in the thick ice. Her crew worked feverishly to free her from an impending frozen death, but despite their efforts, the gradual movement of the unfriendly megaton ice floes soon closed in, crushing the ship's hull and timbers like matchsticks. Shackleton gave the orders to abandon ship and preserve all they could from her.

Now without a ship, the crew camped on ice floes for two months and braved the bitter cold. But the floes were breaking up and drifting in an unfriendly direction, so Shackleton and his men began the slow trek toward the open sea some several hundred miles away. Launching their three tiny lifeboats, on April 19, 1916, they climbed into the small crafts and began rowing for Elephant Island about 100 miles north. Finally, after a perilous journey, they reached their goal, an uninhabited cold rock located about 800 miles from the nearest civilization and human being. With his options narrowing by the hour, Sir Earnest Shackleton made a daring and risky decision. He would take Captain Worsley and four others, climb into a re-rigged lifeboat, and set sail for faraway South Georgia Island. Before Shackleton left, he gathered his men on the beach in subzero weather, looked them in the eyes, and promised each one of them that he would return for them.

With the odds exponentially stacked against them, the remaining 22 men waved goodbye to their beloved captain, perhaps for the last time. Should Shackleton fail in his mission to reach South Georgia, there would be no hope of rescue for his men…ever. No one back home even knew they were there, so no one would know to look for them there.

Miraculously, however, after only 16 days of sailing in wild and furious weather, they sighted land. Eight hundred miles in 16 days! Arriving on South Georgia Island after a terrible storm, their momentary joy turned to dismay and disappointment upon discovering they had landed on the wrong side of the island! Undeterred, Shackleton trudged in waist-deep snow across the island, finally arriving at the whaling village of Stromness. He regrouped and set sail to go retrieve his men, but the treacherous, ice-filled sea wouldn't allow it.

For five long months, huge icebergs blocked the way along with gale-force winds. But suddenly, as if by a miracle, an avenue opened in the ice and Shackleton was able to procure a Chilean vessel, sail through the choppy waters, and make the long journey to Elephant Island.

Upon sighting the beach, there he saw his men, ready and waiting. Captain Worsley peered through his binoculars to do a head count, and remarked to Shackleton, "They're all there, skipper. They're all coming home."

Considering all they had endured, Shackleton lost not a single man. Launching boats from the mother ship, they quickly scrambled aboard and set off for home. No sooner had the ship cleared the island than the ice crashed together behind them.

Contemplating their narrow escape, Shackleton remarked, "It was fortunate you were all packed and ready to go!" It was then that one of his men replied, "We never gave up hope. Whenever the sea was clear of ice, we rolled up our sleeping bags and reminded each other, 'The boss may come today.'"

My friend, at times in life, we may feel like we're stuck on this rock in outer space. Life can be rough. The days can get lonely. The storms may rage. The rains, they do fall. And sometimes, the wind and the cold can mercilessly beat against your heart and your home. And though we are not yet at the end of the world Jesus spoke of, it can certainly feel at times as if the end is near. As we look at the world around us, we might be tempted to give up hope. We might even wonder if Jesus really is coming back like he promised he would.

It is in those moments, as well as in the daily duties of life, that we must "roll up our sleeping bags" and regularly remind ourselves and one another that our Boss may come today!

That is the hope, the blessed hope, that will carry us safely home!

NOTES

WHAT'S SO IMPORTANT ABOUT JESUS' OLIVET DISCOURSE?

1. "A moment of historic danger: It is still 90 seconds to midnight," *Bulletin of the Atomic Scientists*, January 23, 2024, https://thebulletin.org/doomsday-clock/.

CHAPTER 1: WHO IS JESUS OF NAZARETH?—HIS WORDS

1. Shannon Watkins, "Did You Know? The Ignorance of College Graduates," *The James G. Martin Center for Acaemic Renewal*, October 22, 2020, https://www.jamesgmartin.center/2020/10/did-you-know-the-ignorance-of-college-graduates/.

2. J. Warner Wallace, "Is There Any Evidence for Jesus Outside the Bible?," *Cold-Case Christianity*, October 30, 2017, https://coldcasechristianity.com/writings/is-there-any-evidence-for-jesus-outside-the-bible/.

CHAPTER 3: JERUSALEM WILL BE DESTROYED

1. Randall Price, *Rose Guide to the Temple* (Carson, CA: Rose Publishing, 2012), 66.

2. John MacArthur, *The MacArthur Bible Commentary* (Nashville, TN: Thomas Nelson, 2005), 1323.

3. In Matthew 24:31, Jesus does finally gather his elect Jewish brethren from the four corners of the earth at his second coming.

4. Price, *Rose Guide to the Temple*, 99.

CHAPTER 5: WARS WILL BE FOUGHT

1. "US Involvement in War," *Greynun.org*, https://www.greynun.org/wp-content/uploads/2018/10/US-Involvement-in-War.pdf.

2. "Religion Caused Almost Every War in History," *InterVarsity Evangelism*, https://evangelism.intervarsity.org/resource/religion-caused-almost-every-war-history.

3. "Religion Caused Almost Every War in History."

4. Arnold Fruchtenbaum, *Footsteps of the Messiah* (Tustin, CA: Ariel Ministries, 2003), 95-96.

5. Walter Baur, William F. Arndt, F. Wilbur Gingrich, *The Greek-English Lexicon of the New Testament* (Chicago, IL: University of Chicago Press, 1979), 796.

6. Leo Tolstoy, *War and Peace*, https://ourworldindata.org/war-and-peace.

7. Hans Kristensen, Matt Korda, Eliana Johns, Kate Kohn, "Status of World Nuclear Forces," *Federation of American Scientists*, March 31, 2023, https://fas.org/issues/nuclear-weapons/status-world-nuclear-forces/.

8. David Jeremiah, *The World of the End* (Nashville, TN: W Publishing, 2022), 58.

9. Thomas Ice, *Understanding the Olivet Discourse* (Middleton, RI: Stone Tower Press, 2021), 43.

CHAPTER 6: BELIEVERS WILL BE DESPISED

1. Virginia Allen, "Persecution of Christians 'Intense' in Up to 60 Countries Across Globe, Faith Leader Says," *The Daily Signal*, September 6, 2022, https://www.dailysignal.com/2022/09/06/persecution-of-christians-intense-in-up-to-60-countries-across-globe-faith-leader-says/.

2. Aaron Earls, "1 in 7 Global Chirstians Faced Persecution in 2021," *Lifeway Research*, January 28, 2022, https://research.lifeway.com/2022/01/28/1-in-7-global-christians-faced-persecution-in-2021/.

3. Thomas Ice, *Understanding the Olivet Discourse* (Middletown, RI: Stone Tower Press, 2021), 63-64.

CHAPTER 7: LOVE WILL BE SCARCE

1. Geoffrey W. Bromiley, *Theological Dictionary of The New Testament* (Grand Rapids, MI: Eerdmans, 1985), 107.

2. Thomas Ice, *Understanding the Olivet Discourse* (Middletown, RI: Stone Tower Press, 2021), 82.

CHAPTER 9: THE TEMPLE WILL BE DESECRATED

1. 1 Maccabees 1:47-49.

2. 1 Maccabees 1:61.

3. See also Leviticus 25:8.

4. Mark Hitchcock, *The Amazing Claims of Bible Prophecy* (Eugene, OR: Harvest House, 2010), 46.

5. The word *tribulation* is used to describe both the second half of the seven years as well as the entire period—see Revelation 2:22; cf. Matthew 24:10.

CHAPTER 10: THE ANTICHRIST WILL DISPLAY MIRACLES

1. Buist Fanning, *Revelation*, Exegetical Commentary on the New Testament (Grand Rapids: MI: Zondervan, 2020), 377.

2. John explains in Revelation 17:3 that Antichrist's kingdom is made up of "seven heads and ten horns" (Revelation 12:3; 13:1). The ten horns refer to the ten kings (kingdoms) that comprise his global empire (Daniel 2:40-44; 7:24). The seven heads are explained in Revelation 17:10 as "seven kings." Many Bible scholars interpret these to refer to seven worldwide kingdoms through which Satan attempts to rule the world. John states from his perspective and place in history that "five have fallen" (interpreted as Egypt, Babylon, Assyria, Medo-Persia, Greece), "one is" (Rome in John's day), and "the other has not yet come" (Antichrist's kingdom).

CHAPTER 11: THE SON OF MAN WILL DESCEND FROM HEAVEN

1. "General revelation" is traditionally described as God's explanation of himself from the heavens, nature, and through what has been created. Paul claims that what we can learn about the Creator from what has been made is enough evidence for anyone to believe that he exists, and that he is eternally powerful and divine (Romans 1:19-20).

2. Mark Hitchcock, *What Jesus Says About Earth's Final Days* (Sisters, OR: Multnomah, 2003), 81.

3. Revelation 16:14 tells us that the "kings of the whole world," including the "kings of the east" (China), will gather their massive armies at Armageddon (verse 16). We know that these armies will attack Jerusalem (Zechariah 12:1-3; 14:2), and that Christ will slaughter them all. What

is unclear is whether all those armies will "fit" in the geography around Jerusalem, or if some of them are still en route from the Valley of Megiddo (Armageddon) when Jesus meets them. It is conceivable that Jesus' battle with the armies of the earth will extend north of Jerusalem and into the valley. Further, Scripture states that the blood from this battle will either splatter or rise to the level of horses' bridles "for a distance of two hundred miles" (Revelation 14:20).

4. John MacArthur, *Matthew 24–28*, The MacArthur New Testament Commentary (Chicago, IL: Moody, 1989), 51.

CHAPTER 12: THE JEWISH PEOPLE ARE PRESERVED

1. For more detailed historical data on antisemitism during this time, see Olivier Melnick's book, *End-Times Antisemitism* (CreateSpace Independent Publishing Platform, 2018).

2. Dr. Michael Rydelnik, "Is the Modern State of Israel the Fulfillment of Bible Prophecy?," *Chosen People Ministries*, https://www.chosenpeople.com/1s-the-modern-state-of-1srael-2/.

3. Thomas Ice, *Understanding the Olivet Discourse* (Middletown, RI: Stone Tower Press, 2021), 218.

4. Ice, *Understanding the Olivet Discourse*, 224.

CHAPTER 13: THE DAYS OF NOAH ARE REVISITED

1. Andrew Snelling, "Four Lessons from the Mount St. Helens Eruption, *Answers in Genesis*, May 18, 2020, https://answersingenesis.org/geology/four-lessons-mount-st-helens-eruption/.

2. Andy Coghlan, "Massive 'Ocean' Discovered towards Earth's Core," *New Scientist*, June 12, 2014, https://www.newscientist.com/article/dn25723-massive-ocean-discovered-towards-earths-core/.

3. "Archaeologists claim to have found true location of Noah's Ark," *Israel Hayom*, updated April 10, 2021, https://www.israelhayom.com/2021/10/04/archaeologists-claim-to-have-found -true-location-of-noahs-ark/.

4. Gail Labovitz, "Feminist Sexual Ethics Project," https://www.brandeis.edu/projects/fse /judaism/docs/essays/same-sex-marriage.pdf.

5. Labovitz, "Feminist Sexual Ethics Project."

6. Laura Geggel, "Same-Sex Marriage in History: What the Supreme Court Missed," *LiveScience*, May 5, 2015, http://www.livescience.com/50725-same-sex-marriage-history.html.

CHAPTER 14: BE ON THE ALERT

1. Thomas Ice, *Understanding the Olivet Discourse* (Middletown, RI: Stone Tower Press, 2021), 268.

2. In Mark 13:33-37, Jesus repeats "keep on the alert," "stay on the alert," and "be on the alert" four times.

CHAPTER 15: BE A FAITHFUL STEWARD

1. See also Luke 13:34-35; 21:24; Matthew 23:37-39.

CHAPTER 16: BE AWAKE

1. The verse divisions were added in the Old Testament by a Jewish rabbi in AD 1448, and by Robert Estienne in the Greek New Testament in 1551.

2. Arnold G. Fruchtenbaum, *Yeshua: The Life of Messiah from a Messianic Jewish Perspective* (San Antonio, TX: Ariel Ministries, 2022), 481-482.

3. *Leviathan, or The Matter Forme and Power of a Common Wealth Ecclesiastical and Civil*, 1651.

CHAPTER 17: BE WISE WITH WHAT YOU'VE BEEN GIVEN

1. J.R.R. Tolkien, *The Fellowship of the Ring: Being the First Part of The Lord of the Rings*, 50th anniversary ed. (Boston, MA: Houghton Mifflin, 2004), chapter 2, 51.

2. John MacArthur, *Matthew 24–28*, The New Testament Commentary (Chicago, IL: Moody, 1989), 106.

3. "Ancient Money Calculator," *Testament Press*, Testamentpress.com/ancient-money-calculator .html.

4. Dwight Pentecost, *The Words and Works of Jesus Christ* (Grand Rapids, MI: Zondervan, 1981), 409.

5. This poem by C.T. Studd is widely attributed to him, but the original publication in which it first appeared is unknown.

6. Cf. John 7:33; 11:9; 12:35; Galatians 6:10; Ephesians 5:16.

CHAPTER 18: THE JUDGMENT OF THE GENTILES

1. Arnold G. Fruchtenbaum, *Yeshua: The Life of Messiah from a Messianic Jewish Perspective* (San Antonio, TX: Ariel Ministries, 2022), 484.

2. This word (Greek *ethnos*) is used by Matthew 14 times, each time referring to non-Jewish (Gentile) peoples.

3. Biblically, being "sealed" by God signifies protection, authenticity, and ownership, just as it did for those first-century documents that bore the seal of the Roman government (See 1 Kings 21:6-13; Jeremiah 32:10; Daniel 6:17; Matthew 27:62-66; 2 Corinthians 1:21-22; Ephesians 1:13-14).

CHAPTER 19: JESUS OFFERS THE WAY OUT

1. Charles Dickens, *A Tale of Two Cities*, https://www.gutenberg.org/files/98/98-h/98-h.htm.

2. "What is the history of crucifixion?," *Got Questions*, https://www.gotquestions.org/crucifixion .html.

3. "John MacArthur on the cross," *Masterwork Bible Study*, February 26, 2013, https://masterworkss .wordpress.com/2013/02/26/john-macarthur-on-the-cross/.

4. According to church tradition, some of the disciples themselves would also eventually be crucified for their faith in Christ.

5. Jesus also called it "the fiery hell" (Matthew 5:22).

CHAPTER 20: JESUS RESCUES HIS BRIDE FROM THE COMING WRATH

1. Ron Rhodes, *The End Times in Chronological Order* (Eugene, OR: Harvest House, 2012), 223.

OTHER GREAT BOOKS BY JEFF KINLEY

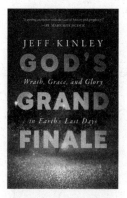

God's Grand Finale examines the characteristics of God that are vividly portrayed in the book of Revelation. As you read, you will develop a clear overview of end-times events, experience how God uses the apocalyptic realities of Revelation to reveal himself to you, and grow in faith as these transformational truths about God deepen your reverence for him.

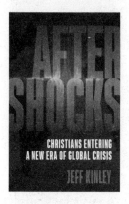

In *Aftershocks*, bestselling author Jeff Kinley reveals how current societal and global trends foreshadow the nearness of the end times—and how the prophecies about what is to come should renew your passion to lovingly proclaim Christ to a suffering world.

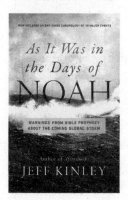

As It Was in the Days of Noah reveals the parallels between the time before the flood and our current culture, highlighting the rise in evil, the surge in immorality, and the pandemic of godlessness. This book equips believers to live wisely, making their days count for eternity.

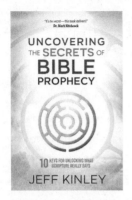

The future may seem like one big mystery—but it doesn't have to be! God has made his plans evident to all. And when you know what he has revealed, you can face the last days with a confident assurance of his provision and victory.

What happens when a country glories in its immorality, turning away from faith in God and obedience to him? This forthright survey of current events and trends offers valuable perspective on the future of America—along with powerful motivation to embrace the only source of lasting hope.

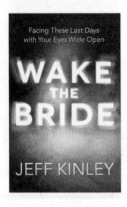

Jesus said, "Wake up and strengthen the things that remain." *Wake the Bride* was written to arouse a sleeping church to prepare for Christ's return. Many are unaware of the signs of the times. Others seem consumed by end-times hype. Jeff Kinley shows that our primary concern should not be the timing of Christ's return, but rather, the spirit and character he desires in his bride. Includes overviews of Jesus and his coming, the church and its mission, heaven and judgment, Satan and the antichrist, and other themes in Revelation.

To learn more about our Harvest Prophecy resources, please visit:

www.HarvestProphecyHQ.com

HARVEST PROPHECY
An Imprint of Harvest House Publishers